Head-First Acting

Published by
Smith and Kraus, Inc.
177 Lyme Road, Hanover, New Hampshire 03755
www.SmithKraus.com

Parts of this book appeared as articles in *Teaching Theatre*,
published by the Educational Theatre Association.

Cover and text design by Julia Hill Gignoux, Freedom Hill Design

First edition: July 2001
10 9 8 7 6 5 4 3 2 1

The Library of Congress Cataloging-In-Publication Data
Miller, Bruce J.
Head-first acting : exercises for drama teachers and students /
by Bruce J. Miller.
p. cm. — (Young actor series)
Includes bibliographical references.
ISBN 1-57525-232-5
1. Acting. I. Title. II. Series.

PN2061 .M465 2001
792'.028—dc21
Library of Congress Control Number: 2001018875

Head-First Acting

A Commonsense Technique for Young Actors

By Bruce J. Miller

Young Actors Series

A SMITH AND KRAUS BOOK

To Joel Friedman,
an alchemist who turned lead into gold every day;
he regularly proved that acting could be taught
as a tangible craft.

Contents

Head-First Acting: An Overview vii

The Basic Tools 1
Look What I Found 1
Gone Fishing 10
Time Bomb 17
Red Light, Green Light 21
The Gunfight 24

Using Physical Actions 37
An Almost Silent Story 38
Add an Action 43
Scenes from the Shower 46
The Solo Shower 46
The Group Shower 49
Pictures at an Exhibition 53
Whisper Down the Lane 60

Conflict and Objectives 70
TYPES OF CONFLICT 70
CONFLICT TO OBJECTIVE 71
The Power Game 72
Stealing Scenes 79
Musical Chairs 88
Murder! 95

Listening and Working Moment to Moment.... 107

Instant Playwriting 111
The Mirror Game 115
The Audio Mirror Game 124
Russian Roulette 125

Using People, Places, and Things 135

USING PROPS AND YOUR BODY TO TELL THE STORY:
  ACTING WITH THE PHYSICAL SELF 136
Hug a Pillow, Slug a Pillow 137
Props and Common Senses 144
Character Business 145
USING CATEGORIES: ANALYSIS THROUGH RELATIONSHIP
  AND LOCATION 147
Difficult Relationships 149
Two-Line Dramas 152

Language and Style 159

Announcer Training 160
The Children's Book 162
Pledge of Allegiance 165
When I Went to the Store, I Bought 170

Using the Script 181

Monologue Makers 183
Scenes Without Content 190

Afterword 201

Glossary 204

Bibliography 208

Head-First Acting: An Overview

"What is it you're doing here?" I gently ask the beginning actor early in the semester. I have just interrupted a monologue she is delivering.

"I'm crying," my young actor responds. She is surprised at my need to interrupt her with a question so obvious.

"And doing it very well, too, I must say. But why are you crying?"

"Because my character is sad," she answers.

"Ah-ha!" I say. "Good! But what about the words you're saying while you're crying? What are you trying to get by saying them? Why has your character chosen to say those particular things at this particular time to the particular person she is speaking to, I wonder?"

"I'm not sure," the actor admits.

"I bet the playwright knew the answers to all those questions, and the answers are probably important," I casually offer. "I suspect that playwright worked very hard to get those words just right. So it may not be a good idea to let your crying swallow those words up."

"I see what you mean," the actor says sheepishly. "I was having problems with the dialogue."

Even when you pointedly ask beginning actors about the work they are doing onstage at any given moment, they will almost invariably start to tell you what their characters are feeling. An actor's primary focus, however, should be on what that character is doing—not on what she is feeling. It is a character's actions that an audience can see and understand. It is a character's actions that allow an audience to know what is going on in the story being presented; and it is only through the combined actions of all the characters in a play that the story laid out in the script gets told.

An audience may, for a short time, be able to appreciate the fact that an actor can conjure up seemingly real tears and cry at will or muster up enough anger to single-handedly destroy an enemy army. But once these abilities have been shared with an audience, the audience quickly grows weary of them and soon turns its attention elsewhere. Audience members can never see directly into the hearts and minds of a play's characters. They can only determine a character's thoughts and feelings as a result of what that character does and says. What an audience wants, what it has come to the theater for in the first place, is the story.

It is an actor's job, then, to tell stories clearly, dramatically, and believably. The best acting will always serve the play in which the actor is performing. It is not enough that an actor comes off well to an audience. A good actor must come to accept his responsibility for bringing to life the work of the playwright. When the play is worthy, the actor will best serve himself and the production by paying close attention to what the playwright has provided.

Good actors constantly use their brains to make the best dramatic choices at every moment of their work—in the beat, in the scene, and in the play as a whole. It is only after actors make and explore these choices that artistic freedom comes, and it is this freedom that permits the seeming spontaneity apparent in fine acting.

Even a beginning acting student can tell you that it is the actor's job to be believable. But what they will seldom tell you is that a good actor must also be able to make choices—choices that help them tell the best possible story while serving the playwright's script. This three-pronged definition of good acting can serve as a compass for actors in all their work and keep them from getting lost in the densest theatrical forest. It is also the basic principle behind this book and is the reason that I call it *Head-First Acting*. Emoting alone will not tell that story, but carrying out actions, actions appropriate for the story being told, will.

This book provides teachers and students of acting with tools for developing useful, lasting techniques for teaching and learning the craft of acting. The basics of acting craft are introduced, developed, and reinforced incrementally through practical exercises for the actor's mind and body. The concepts and exercises offered here instill in actors an understanding of the craft that can be effectively applied later to more structured acting work. Although explanations of the concepts and the exercises are directed toward teachers of acting, students of acting will certainly profit from reading them. Even if individual readers cannot immediately play the group exercises described, thinking them through and understanding the implications they hold for actors can be profitable. Further, with a bit of imagination many of the exercises can be adapted for individual or small group use.

Head-First Acting offers practical ways of thinking about the acting process and its connection to making good theater or film. The acting process and the making of good theater are interconnected, a point not often emphasized in today's actor training. It is ultimately the actor's job to serve the play and production in which he appears; therefore, an understanding of how a play works is as important as any other acting tool an actor may learn.

The inspiration for this book was personal. During my own acting training, I often found myself thrown into exercises that may have been fascinating but proved of little practical worth. How I had become a better actor for having done the exercises often eluded me. Was I better able to examine a script and make compelling and organic choices? Was I more facile when trying to please that demanding director who couldn't communicate what he needed from me? Was my acting more interesting, more exciting, more clear? Regrettably, the time and energy I spent doing the acting exercises assigned me during my years of training was time and energy wasted. Too often there was simply no direct or even indirect transference from an exercise to my development as an actor. Sometimes the problem was the exercise itself. Other times it was a matter of faulty teaching—an inability of the instructor to bridge the gap between the exercise and the useful acting technique it was supposed to demonstrate. For most actors, certainly for actors here in the United States, acting results from interpreting a script. Most actors spend their careers making choices and then playing actions or saying dialogue based on that script. If the training exercises don't focus on these primary aspects of acting, then what is their value?

The time students spend in theater class is limited, to say the least. What most teachers and students want are meat-and-potato exercises—exercises that can quickly make a difference. That is what the reader will find here. I have made up some of the exercises; others I developed from earlier versions presented to me. Each has proved enormously helpful to my students, and I continue to use them in my own studio work. For new student actors, the exercises found here should provide empirical proof that basic technique is both essential and possible to obtain with practice. For veteran students, they should provide an effective reminder that basic craft remains the cornerstone of all good acting work. The acting points contained in these exercises transfer clearly and easily into many of the acting situations in which actors find themselves. For each exercise presented, I provide a clearly rendered explanation of purpose, a step-by-step set of instructions for carrying out the exercise, and a detailed explanation of the acting theory behind it. Teachers are also provided with helpful ideas and likely scenarios that will better prepare them for trying the exercises with their classes. For readers unfamiliar with acting lingo, the glossary at the back of the book gives basic explanations of acting terms and concepts.

The exercises cover the basics that actors will continue to use as their work grows in sophistication and subtlety. But as

David Mamet once put so well, "Acting is simple. It just ain't easy." Though the tools of the acting trade are few, for many of us they take a lifetime to master. Here you will find exercises that deal with the playing objectives, the use of the "magic if" and logical sequence, the building of character through action, and the actor as storyteller—all basics that I consider tremendously important. Students will need to think about stakes, given circumstances, and conflict. They will need to concern themselves with listening and moment-to-moment work as well as through-lines of action. In short, they will need to think about all the things actors must think about when they are dealing with a script. These exercises really do work. If used in the manner outlined, students will quickly begin to build a technique. My hope is that both teachers and students will find them as effective as I have. I am always interested in feedback, so let me know how they work for you. I can be reached at brucejmill@aol.com.

The Basic Tools

An audience comes to the theater to see a compelling story—one that makes them suspend their disbelief and be carried off into the world of the play. Without thinking, an audience senses a good story, or, as the case may be, one that doesn't work. An audience is pulled into a plot that is well developed—one with a beginning, middle, and end, and lots of exciting conflict in between. It is no coincidence then, that successful playwrights write those kinds of plays. A successful play has characters who carry out interesting actions—actions that cause and develop conflict, which in turn create the good stories those playwrights have set out to produce. But a play script provides only the skeleton of a fully realized production. It is the actor's job to put meat on the bone by adding to the story suggested in the script. Here is an exercise that both encapsulates and demonstrates all this. I call it Look What I Found.

Look What I Found

Purpose

This exercise clearly demonstrates that actors are responsible for far more than simply being believable. Your students will learn that good acting requires them to make choices that are not only believable, but interesting as well. Choices that enhance the script—the source material for their selected actions. In addition, your students will discover, as the exercise progresses, that even "interesting" is not enough for good actors. It will become apparent to them that they, as actors, are also responsible for telling the most compelling story possible. Ultimately, they will realize that, like the playwrights who provide the raw material for their work, actors are responsible for inventing, as well as executing, the story that the playwright blueprints. Your students will come to realize that they, as well as the playwright, must take responsibility for telling a good story.

Method

The instructions for Look What I Found should be kept spare and simple. That way your students will have the opportunity to use or fail to use their common sense to find solutions to the problems presented. Just ask them to come up with a story (it need not be longer than a minute or two) centered around an object you will place on the floor. The stories they present should have no dialogue, and the only character involved in the story should be the one they play. There should be no invisible or imagined characters interacting with the student performing; this will only detract from the audience's ability to see, understand, and believe what is going on.

After each presentation, your class should report on and discuss the stories they saw or failed to see. They should not be permitted to make assumptions about, interpolate, extrapolate, or add to what they actually saw. Each performing student must be solely responsible for creating all necessary aspects of the story presented. What the audience sees or fails to see is the responsibility of the student doing the exercise. The actor's job, then, is to come up with choices that will make her story both clear and compelling. When all comments have been heard and discussed, the actual performers should tell the story they acted out specifically. A further discussion should then center on what was seen and understood, what was not, and, most important, why. It is a good idea to let all actors rethink their work once their pieces have been discussed and to allow them to redo their work incorporating the feedback given them. As my favorite English teacher used to remind us, the real work is in the rewriting. So it is with actors as well—in the redoing.

The objects used in the story are up to you, but the exercise works best when the props used increase in dramatic potential. I often start with a penny, go to a quarter or a dollar in the next round, and finally present the actors with a wallet. For later rounds, more dramatic objects could be a stack of twenty-dollar bills, a baby doll representing an actual infant, or a realistic-looking play gun. These high-stake props often lead to fascinating scenarios.

Though acting doesn't require Mensa thinking, actors nonetheless abandon whatever native intelligence they possess once they leave their seats and become actors onstage. The exercise described here requires your students to use their intelligence—to choose actions that tell a story in a sequential, logical, and believable fashion. Since the actors also serve as their own playwrights, the exercise requires them to take on the responsibility of creating the best possible story even when the central object is as insignificant as a penny might appear to be—when not given the proper storytelling consideration. Look What I Found also puts your students in the position of having to balance the creation of an interesting story with the obligation of keeping the story clear and believable.

ROUND 1

In the first round of the exercise, it is important to use an object that has little overt dramatic potential. This will force your students immediately into the head-first mode, or quickly lure them into the acting trap created by the setup of the exercise.

I usually start out by placing a penny on the playing area. After instructing the class to take a few moments to come up with a wordless story centered on the penny, an enthusiastic volunteer shoots a hand into the air. More times than not this trailblazer calls "scene!" and simply crosses the stage without glancing at the penny. When the actor again calls "scene!" at the finish, he proudly turns toward me for my response. I tell my actor that it wasn't a very interesting story. The actor usually tells me that a penny is not a very interesting subject. I then tell him that it is up to him to make an interesting story with the penny—that he is the actor as storyteller. If I let the actor redo his work, the second time he might glance at the penny but continue on to the end, still not conflicted. I then tell him that his story is now improved because of the contact between him and the coin, but the work is still not compelling. He might then tell me that his story represents what he would do if he saw a penny in the street, and since he wanted to keep the work believable, he chose to do no more than glance at that little red Lincoln-head.

The struggle between believability and compelling drama is an ongoing one for any actor, but one necessary to engage in every acting situation. As the discussion continues, your students will begin to get the idea that creating a good story goes along with maintaining believability. As your actors take turns performing the exercise, they will build on what they have learned from the discussion follow-ups. Once they get the hang of the importance of story, someone invariably chooses to react to finding the penny as though it were a priceless ancient coin or, perhaps, the Hope diamond. This thrusts the acting discussion in a new direction. We now have a dramatic event occurring, but one that no audience would believe for even a moment. Who gets so excited over a penny?

The discussion eventually brings out the fact that the actor making a big deal about finding the penny had the right story-telling idea, but had not justified the action in his story so that the audience would believe his reactions. In time, your students will come to solve the problem by making the penny a valuable one, but, of course, their acting choices will have to demonstrate sequentially how the character onstage came to know that it is.

The successful exercise that evolves will have a clear beginning, middle, and end, with moments of discovery and/or victory and defeat, specifically executed and clearly rendered for the audience. The audience will understand enough about the character to know why the character stopped for and examined the coin and what the results of the examination were. The most common scenarios that evolve include:

A coin collector sees the penny, examines it, and discovers it is valuable.

A superstitious person sees the coin and checks for whether the head is up.

A person needing change searches the sidewalk and finds the penny.

A coin collector sees the penny, examines it, and discovers it is valuable, but can't get it off the pavement because it is somehow stuck.

The last scenario builds on a solid conflict—the struggle to free the valuable penny—and can lead to a very satisfying story, either dramatic or comic. When well done, the story remains believable, but the actor as storyteller has truly taken that formerly boring penny to dramatic heights not perceived without the use of *Head-First Acting*.

The storytelling issues that your actors must resolve include:

How does the story allow for and justify the character's interest in a penny?

Do we know enough about the character to believe in his actions?

Does the encounter with the penny lead to victory or defeat, and why?

Will the audience be satisfied with the event they witnessed because the story offered up to them creates a sense of completion?

Will there be lingering questions, loose ends, or blanks left for the audience to fill in? When there are not, chances are the story will feel complete and satisfying for the audience watching.

ROUND 2

Using a quarter or even a dollar bill after the exercise with a penny may prove difficult for your students. Though a quarter and a dollar bill are more valuable finds, essentially neither of them offers a life-changing opportunity. It's obviously nicer to find a dollar bill than a penny, but dramatically speaking, the terrain is not that different. Your students may struggle to make up a story that will hold an audience after witnessing umpteen variations with the penny. Because of that, you will probably see several pieces of work that are plot thick but very thin in believ-ability and clarity. Eventually though, you should be able to lead your class to the conclusion that a full, simple, and believable reaction to finding the dollar bill will provide an audience with a sense of completion and satisfaction. In other words, one big, real "Hey! I found a whole dollar!" moment is sometimes all an actor can and should do, and the decision to execute that kind of moment is far more compelling than creating an outlandish story, or one that cannot be deciphered by the audience. And, of course, a well-acted moment onstage is never something to be sneered at.

ROUND 3

Now finding a wallet is a whole new ball game. Suddenly, the story involves ethical issues and is therefore interesting in and of itself. Your actors will have to work far less hard creating a story that will hold an audience. The viewers will automatically want to know how the characters onstage will react to the temptation star-ing them in the face. Whether the actors as characters choose to take the wallet for themselves, take it with the intention of trying to find the rightful owner, or leave it where it is, the story of the journey to that decision will hold the audience if it is clearly exe-cuted. The actors must convey the internal struggle through their physical actions, since no dialogue is permitted in the exercise.

You'll probably want to point out that since this round has a much stronger built-in dramatic situation to build from, the acting assignment is actually easier than in previous rounds. You might want to remind your students that scripts almost always contain these interesting dramatic situations, but it is the actor's responsibility to read a script in such a way that those built-in dramatic hooks become apparent to them. Learning to suck out the good stuff in a self-made script now will come in handy later when your students try to do the same thing with an actual playwright's work.

Even in the earlier rounds of this game, the topic of given circumstances will probably come up as a useful tool to tell the story. Obviously, the *who* and *what* (the character and situation in the story) will be discussed. Combined, they create the central dramatic situation. But the *where* and *when* will probably be given far less consideration. In the wallet scenario these two W's take on great importance in terms of getting across the thinking process of the *who* presented by your actors.

Here is an example of what I mean. Suppose the scene takes place in a public area—on a busy city sidewalk, for instance. An area with heavy traffic will certainly affect the actions taken by the character whether he has honest intentions or not. After all, the character can be seen. If the character's intentions are honest, for instance, action will have to be taken quickly before a less honest person spies the potential treasure. If the character is dishonest but careful, she may want to check out the wallet without being seen before deciding to take it, whereas a more impulsive thief might just grab it. Whatever the choices your actors come up with, they will have to create a step-by-step scenario that establishes the location of the action and makes clear the inner process of the character.

The same considerations must be applied to time of day, time of year, climate, and period in time the action takes place. Nighttime, for example, makes it easier for criminals to fulfill their desires. Winter in a northern climate changes what characters might be wearing and will therefore affect their ability to conceal stolen property and their willingness to hang out before taking conclusive action. Turn-of-the-last-century behavior might be different than that displayed in the late twentieth century. You get the idea. Each choice can and will color the actions and change the palette of colors with which your actors paint their story. As storytellers, they should be encouraged to think with plenty of detail. The more specific their decisions about given circumstances, the more freedom they will have from moment to moment because their chosen actions will be far less generalized.

LATER ROUNDS

A gun shining in the morning sun on a busy sidewalk. A crying baby lying in a deserted alleyway. A stack of crisp twenty-dollar bills screaming to be picked up by a lucky passerby. Each of these setups practically begs for a big reaction from the individual who sees them. Can your actors meet the expectations of the waiting audience believably and compellingly? That is the challenge presented in these later rounds.

The big, reactive choice that is full and believable yet demonstrates the surprise of the moment in a spontaneous manner is an incredibly difficult feat for an actor. In addition, this seemingly spontaneous moment must be executed as part of an ongoing story communicated through a sequence of specific actions. Managing to do all this requires great skill and, not unlikely, a lot of rehearsing. Too often young actors believe that good acting is an innate intuitive talent that springs forth fully realized. Juggling the requirements of these advanced versions of Look What I Found can go a long way toward dispelling that notion. Learning to find, control, and believably repeat the big reactive moments will certainly challenge your young actors. These later rounds will also go a long way toward proving to your students that actors, like most artists, work very hard to achieve their desired results.

To demonstrate the difficulty of the seemingly spontaneous big reaction, I often begin the later rounds with the gun exercise. I ask a volunteer actor to leave the room or to cover his eyes. I then place a real-looking prop gun in the playing area and tell my waiting actor that when he is ready, he should call scene, enter the playing area, and simply react to whatever he finds.

Invariably, when the actor enters the playing area and sees the gun, his shock and surprise is so spontaneous and real that it instantly becomes a classic moment of good acting. Unfortunately, the acting seems real not because the brilliant young actor has generated a De Niro moment but because it *is* real. In fact, it is not acting at all. The student is shocked to see a seemingly real gun lying on the floor and has simply responded. On the one hand, spontaneously responding fully and honestly is the goal of all fine actors, but on the other, actors must be able to repeat that moment, performance after performance. When asked to repeat the exercise, almost without fail the young actor tries to re-create the previous spontaneous reaction and completely fails to make the audience believe it.

Introducing the later rounds in this fashion provides your actors with an example of the big choice all of them should aspire to. Clearly, this kind of acting is the best kind. It is clear, believable, compelling, and certainly creates moment after moment of fine storytelling. Keeping that spontaneous reaction in mind, your students should then try to build up their individual story lines as specifically as possible, using the given circumstances available to them. They will want to create a story with a clear beginning, middle, and end, one with a clearly defined conflict and resolution. They will also need to find a way to make the big moments, when they arrive, fully realized and believable, either through some personal inner process or through the physical actions they have used to create their work in the earlier rounds.

Wrap-up

Once you have taken your students through a few rounds of this exercise, they will have certainly developed an understanding of the concepts you have been using with them. At this point it might be worthwhile to give the exercise as a prepared assignment, one that can be planned step by step and rehearsed in a proper manner until all the details are mastered. That way it becomes the obligation of your actors to bring in polished work that is clear and compelling and that believably tells the best possible story. Doing so will, of course, require head-first work.

Gone Fishing

Did you ever notice that there are not a lot of novels and films about fishing? Movies such as *The Perfect Storm* and *Jaws* may include fishing scenes, but for dramatic punch they rely on special effects and various other plot elements. Yes, of course, there is *The Old Man and the Sea*—a novel about those primal struggles of man against a worthy adversary, man against nature, and man against himself. But most fish are far less exciting to reel in than the one old Santiago mixed it up with. Then there's *Moby Dick,* if we consider a whale a fish, but that was a fish of unusual dimensions pursued by a captain with an equally huge obsession. The only other fishing novel I can think of offhand is *A River Runs Through It,* made into a beautiful film by director Robert Redford. But, though Brad Pitt was in the lead, the film was not a commercial success, and for many viewers, the film, like fishing itself, was boring—too internal and more about waiting than about primal emotions, conflict, and personal obsession.

It is the basic nature of the "bait and wait" pastime that makes Gone Fishing an excellent exercise for a beginning acting class at the start of a semester. It reiterates and makes clear some of the points referred to in the previous exercise and gives your students a chance to review the lessons about acting presented in Look What I Found.

Purpose
Gone Fishing reinforces the concept that, along with believability, good acting requires an actor to tell a good story—one

that has a beginning, middle, and end and an engaging conflict that holds the story together. The exercise also emphasizes that acting, though it may look like real life when it's well done, is not random or haphazard, as life sometimes is. On the contrary, acting requires selection and control. Whether actors are interpreting a play or creating one extemporaneously, they must function as playwrights, continually making choices that tell a good story and keep it moving at all times.

Method

ROUND 1

For the first round, ask for several volunteers. Five or six will work nicely in a class of twenty, but do what's comfortable in your teaching space. Make sure that each of your fishers has enough room to work in and that all can be seen clearly by the class. Tell your fishers to go into the playing area and space themselves so that each has an equal amount of space to work in. Instruct your actors that, even though they can see their fellow actors, they are to act as if they are alone. Also instruct them that this is to be a nonverbal exercise, so all acting must be done without dialogue; they may make sounds if necessary or desirable, but no words can be used to help their acting or to make the story clearer. Tell your actors that when you give the signal, they are to go fishing using only their playing area and imagination to fill in the details. Just before beginning, instruct the rest of your class to watch carefully because a discussion will follow. Try to allow all of the fishing actors to play out their story before ending the exercise, but use your own instincts to determine when the exercise should draw to a close. Obviously, if what is happening onstage is interesting, let it continue. However, if you find that the action onstage is not interesting enough to keep it running much longer, side coach by saying "five minutes left!" or "one minute to go!" Also tell your actors that when they have finished their exercise, they should exit the playing area and that their exit should be considered part of their story.

DISCUSSION

This exercise reinforces that definition of good acting as acting that is believable and that tells the best possible story while serving the script. Fishing, because it is generally regarded as uneventful, intentionally sets a trap for the beginning actor who doesn't realize that the best acting requires good storytelling as well as believability. Many of your committed actors will probably make believable choices that are focused and specific. Several will no doubt be able to sequence a set of choices that makes logical sense and therefore contains a throughline of action. But for many of your fishing actors, the majority of the actions they choose will ultimately add up to a dull presentation because, in the minds of those students, fishing is dull. The point here is that presentations that are not only believable but exciting to watch on an ongoing or continuous basis are the ones that work best.

When the exercise is over, ask your audience what they thought. They might begin with what they liked and what they didn't. Try to guide the discussion so that your students make a distinction between what they liked and what worked dramatically, the latter being more appropriate for the discussion. Ask the class which actor they spent the most time watching and why. Your class will find that their attention and focus shifted to whomever was doing the most interesting thing at any particular moment. However, those who create a sequence of actions, or throughline, that compels the viewers' attention are more likely to maintain the focus of an audience, even when something interesting begins to happen elsewhere. In your discussion, make sure you survey the class to determine which actors they watched at a particular time and which ones they watched consistently. Ultimately, though the focus may shift from time to time, those that have the most interesting throughline will have gotten the most attention, and the audience will have followed those stories the most closely. In addition, most of the class will be able to retell those stories with the fewest gaps, which emphasizes the fact that an audience watches actions onstage that tell a story and not necessarily those that are the most realistic.

Those in your class who enact a sequence of actions that results from given circumstances or create obstacles that must be overcome will be the most successful. The combination of manipulating a given circumstance and/or overcoming obstacles will provide the catalyst for strong conflict, which is, of course, the engine of good drama. The trick here is maintaining believability while engaging in conflicts. Some beginning actors, in the cause of telling a good story, will sacrifice reality and go over the top by overacting. These actors have not yet learned that a good story believably told requires no extra mustard. They have not yet mastered the difference between suggesting an action and really committing to it. You will need to point out the difference when this occurs. You may choose to do so as a side comment or during the discussion that follows the exercise. Your beginning students must learn to distinguish between filling a moment and indicating it, or bad acting habits will develop. This threat is particularly dangerous in the beginning stages of actor training.

The students whose work combines believability with good storytelling should be highlighted, for they are the models for all the work that follows. The lessons learned from these early exercises will lay the grounding principles for the scene work that lies in wait around the bend. It is important that from the beginning of their training your students understand that a good play is never about the ordinary. On the contrary, a good play always focuses on that special time when even the ordinary, slowly or suddenly, develops into a climactic situation of some kind. This is true whether a play is character or plot driven. Something extraordinary must occur if the play is to be dramatically successful. If students can get this axiom into their basic perception of dramatic work now, their ability to discern the drama innately contained in a play script will be greatly enhanced. In turn this basic concept will better enable them to make choices that will serve them as actors as well as the script they are working from.

So, what are some of the obstacles and given circumstances

that can turn a boring day of fishing into a whale of a story? Let's start with given circumstances—the who, what, when, and where of acting. Under the *who* category, fear can be an effective magnet for conflict. Suppose the who is afraid of touching bait, getting wet, touching a fish, or getting hooked? Under the *what* category, suppose the character is hungry, or a beginner, or a young child, or without proper equipment? Under the *when* category, suppose it is winter, or summer, or a hundred years ago, a thousand years ago, a million years ago? Suppose it is nighttime or dawn? Under the *where* category, suppose the character is standing in a lake, in breaking ocean waves, on a dock, in a boat, or on ice? Each of these factors can be manipulated and combined to produce situations marvelous for dramatic action filled with conflict and laden with obstacles to overcome. Remember, one purpose of this exercise is to get your student actors thinking in these terms.

Here are some more obstacles that might help a struggling fishing actor become more interesting onstage. Every one of these obstacles, and countless more that could be uncovered, comes as a result of considering some of the basic storytelling conflicts that can be associated with the fishing situation. These include person against nature and person against herself. The most common and effective dramatic conflict, person against person, is not really available in the fishing exercise—simply because the instructions for the exercise required a working-alone scenario. However, the possibilities are still vast. Consider, for instance, the possibilities of environmental conditions. Suppose it is raining, snowing, or windy? What's the mosquito or fly factor? Is the water rough or calm? How about using boredom as an enemy? Or fatigue? Staying awake can be an interesting obstacle to overcome. How about seasickness or the sun? Your students will get ideas from watching their peers or from the discussion that follows their presentation. You may want to brainstorm after the first round, so that the next group has an array of possibilities firmly in hand before they begin Round 2.

ROUND 2

The second round of this exercise is played out exactly as the first. However, the fishing actors will be far better equipped for telling a good story. What they have learned through observation in the first round in combination with the possible suggestions that came from the discussion that followed will provide all the basic equipment necessary for some excellent fishing tales. Follow the same procedure as in the first round, but warn your observing students that they will be kept far busier trying to keep up with the various stories unfolding than they were in the previous round because more good stories will be told this time through.

DISCUSSION

The big challenge in the second round is whether your students will be able to convert their chosen given circumstances, obstacles, and conflicts into good throughlines of action. Will they be able to sequence their choices into coherent and dramatically effective stories? There may be an undesirable tendency in this round by some of your actors to punch up their work in a way that will guarantee that the audience watches. This is what I call the "creeping ham factor," and if you see it developing in any presented work, you should point it out to the guilty performing parties—immediately, if possible. These scene-stealing efforts usually result because your actors now know that watchability is one of the criteria for success. To ensure they are interesting, or as interesting as the fishing actor next door, there is a temptation to go overboard, to overdo it. Again, developing and maintaining a sense of what comes off as real is an extremely important skill for a young actor to develop, so any effort to grab focus at the expense of believability must be thwarted.

Over all, the performers in this round will probably provide a three-ring circus of fishing scenarios. It will be difficult for audience members to decide on which fishing actor to focus their attention, so a discussion of where and when focus shifted will be interesting and enlightening. A well-conducted discussion can point up what kind of work draws and holds an audience's attention, as well as why. In addition, there will probably be a variety of styles and genres displayed in the exercises this time through.

The given circumstances and obstacles that each actor chooses to employ will create a particular kind of story and therefore require a particular manner of storytelling to bring it off successfully. An exercise focusing on an attack by flies could either be frightening, if the flies are ferocious and their bites hurt, or extremely funny. The manner in which the actions are executed should let the audience know the kind of story they are watching. For it to be funny, the actions the actor selects must be done in such a way that the audience has permission to laugh. That will require a particular manner or style in executing the action. A misunderstanding of the story being created could lead an actor to make choices that do not work effectively or to execute those choices in a way that hinders effective storytelling.

Wrap-up

The discussion will have, hopefully, brought to your students' attention considerations that had not occurred to them while they were working. You might want to give them another opportunity to do the exercise after the discussion, or you might want to assign it as homework, enabling them to rehearse and polish their presentations. Now that your students have seen how the exercise works, it might be beneficial for them to start from scratch and think through the entire scenario from entrance to exit. Repeating the exercise will reinforce that reworking, as with most skills, develops craft more than haphazard inspiration. Allowing your students to work through the whole process will produce a much-improved product and a stronger more efficient process as well. And that is, after all, what actor training is all about. Developing in your students the ability to analyze and work through any given dramatic material so that the material is well served, or even enhanced, should be a primary goal.

Time Bomb

A good story has a throughline of action as Look What I Found clearly demonstrated. This throughline of action, or *arc,* as it is sometimes called, is dependent on a story's built-in conflict. In the previous exercises, when student actors failed to create or recognize the potential or real conflicts available to them, they missed an essential opportunity to deliver a good story. More often than not, however, a playwright builds into her script a story line that has one or more clearly delineated conflicts that an actor can and must build on. In the exercise that follows, your students will learn to apply some of the basic tools of acting that stem directly from the recognition of conflict and its relationship to the characters involved in that conflict.

Purpose

The purpose of this exercise is at least threefold. First, it demonstrates to beginning actors that doing is far better than being: having something specific to do gives purpose to action and relieves self-consciousness as well. Second, it demonstrates that playing a strong, clear, specific objective allows the actor to fully commit to any action and makes the pretend aspect of acting more real. Third, it demonstrates that the more important the actor can make the objective, the more exciting the work will be for both the actor and the audience. In addition, the actor will probably find that by making the stakes high, the likelihood of producing spontaneous, exciting, and honest emotional work is greatly increased.

Method

There are three rounds in this game. Directions should be clearly stated before each round, but explanations should be minimized. Only when each round has been completed by the actors, should a detailed discussion begin focusing on what each individual actor thought and felt while working and what was observed while watching others work.

ROUND 1

Tell your actors to go to one end of the working area. The instructor should sit in a chair at the opposite end of the space. I have found that an auditorium or theater works beautifully for this exercise, particularly if the space has steps that lead to the instructor's position. If no steps are available, then other physical obstacles such as chairs may be placed between the students and instructor. A large area is best. I have even done the exercise outdoors on a hill, seating myself at the top or at the bottom. Both variations produce interesting results. Don't be afraid to be creative.

Inform your actors that they are to walk toward you, one at a time, maintaining eye contact until the exercise is completed. If for any reason they should lose eye contact, they are out. At that time the next actor will begin his walk. If an actor maintains eye contact for the entire journey, his exercise is completed only when he shakes your extended hand— eyes, of course, still squarely on yours.

DISCUSSION

You will find that most of your actors will display enormous self-consciousness. It is no easy task to remain comfortable locking eyes with the instructor while the class watches, particularly if the exercise is attempted at the beginning of a semester. There will probably be lots of giggling and side commentary. Discourage this if necessary during the exercise, but discuss the reasons for it after the exercise is completed. Ask your students to give examples of discomfort they witnessed or felt. You'll probably get plenty. Remind actors they'll want to get rid of these physical giveaways. It is likely that your students will cop to nervousness and self-consciousness resulting from feeling naked and clumsy during the seemingly long, long journey across the work space.

ROUND 2

Repeat the game, but with the following addition. Tell your actors that you are sitting above a bomb ready to go off. In the fashion of the movie, *Speed,* the bomb will go off if for any reason eye contact is lost. The mission is completed only when each actor in turn has grasped your outstretched hand. Help the exercise along by blowing up if eye contact is broken and be sure to give heartfelt thanks when a mission is successful. Remember, their acting will be better if they have you to react to.

DISCUSSION

You will probably find a different group of actors at the end of this round. Your students' body language will likely communicate very different things this time through. Both their pace and strength of movement and their commitment to the exercise will be vastly improved. They will be excited as individuals and as a group. Solicit reactions from your actors. They will eventually tell you the change resulted because they were focused on you rather than on themselves and that having a strong purpose for their journey removed their self-consciousness. Their focus will have been totally on the work, not on themselves.

ROUND 3

This round is played the same way as the previous one, but with this addition: Not only will the bomb go off if eye contact is lost, but it will go off in a proscribed amount of time even with eye contact maintained. Make sure that you give them little time to get to you. Count aloud to increase the suspense and make adjustments in the tempo of your count to insure maximum life-and-death stakes. Try to make the bomb as real for you as it is for your actors.

In all probability you will see actors doing thing physically, up those stairs or around those other obstacles, that you never dreamed you would see them do. I have seen nerds become Errol Flynns, and the fashion models in the class break their nails trying to save me from going up in smoke.

It will be obvious that the time element increases the stakes of the situation and eliminates any possibilities for thought and planning during the exercise. Everyone will completely give themselves up to the moment because the task allows for nothing else. As a result, this round will be the most exciting to watch and to do. Further, because everything other than the objective will be completely spontaneous, the action will have the immediacy of a sporting event or of reality itself. All acting will be reacting—tripping on steps, struggling to stand while maintaining eye contact, negotiating steps in twos and threes, even reacting to the exploding bombs that mark each failed attempt will be full and completely in the moment. The handshake that follows each completed victorious mission will be as heartfelt as Forrest Gump's with JFK. In short, there will be "the thrill of victory and the agony of defeat."

Wrap-up

This exercise serves as a wonderful metaphor for the acting process itself and for the basic technique that you should try hard to instill in your actors. Saving their lives and escaping the clutches of death provides a strong acting objective. The risk and danger (stakes) in completing their mission is huge, and the time element imposed on them insures they will employ only essential honest actions. As a result, the scene that plays itself out will be simple, clear, believable, and dramatic. Not every acting situation offers this ultimate life-and-death scenario, but it is essential that the young actor develop the skills to make every acting moment as close to this ideal as possible. For only then will her work shine with honesty and excitement. Only then will the actor truly bring to dramatic life that scripted blueprint provided by the playwright.

Red Light, Green Light

For some teachers, Time Bomb, with its suggestion of violence, might not be a comfortable or appropriate activity. If this is the case, the children's game, Red Light, Green Light, though clearly different in nature, offers an opportunity to introduce similar acting principles along with one or two unique to itself.

Purpose

Properly set up, Red Light, Green Light, like the Time Bomb exercise, demonstrates that doing on-stage is far better than simply being. The game also demonstrates that when actors play an objective strongly and clearly, the pretend becomes almost real—in spite of the fact that the stakes are certainly not as high as in Time Bomb. Obviously when the stakes are life and death, dramatic situations are the most compelling. What this exercise does demonstrate, which Time Bomb does not, is that when actors follow preconceived notions, they can miss opportunities for exciting dramatic choices.

Method

As in Time Bomb, this game can be played in several stages. Directions should be clearly stated before each round with minimal explanation. When the round has been completed, a discussion should cover observations, thoughts, and feelings.

ROUND 1

Play Round 1 of Time Bomb, as described earlier, emphasizing that self-consciousness stems from the actors' lack of external purpose in the activity.

ROUND 2

For Round 2, the game of Red Light, Green Light is introduced and explained. One person is "it" and stations herself a good distance from the rest of the group. The opposing players line up side by side, facing "it" along a predetermined horizontal line; this line is home base. When "it" calls out "green light," she turns away from the other players who then advance toward her, the object being to tag her. As soon as she calls out "red light," she turns back and faces the others in an attempt to catch someone moving. Anyone she sees moving is sent back to home base. When someone reaches and tags "it," the game is over.

DISCUSSION

The discussion should proceed from an analysis of the game itself to its relevance to the acting process. That should always be a rule of thumb in an acting class. Games should never be seen by students as just games. Students must always relate the game being played to acting. The teacher must make sure this transference happens; otherwise games are not helpful tools.

During the discussion, students will likely discover that the game was more exciting to play for those who took the most chances. Those same people were, no doubt, the most interesting to watch as well. This is an extremely important acting concept. Actors who try hard to obtain their acting objective do interesting and exciting work. Whether they achieve that objective is irrelevant because that is predetermined by the script—not by the actor's intensity in pursuit. However, the degree of risk and commitment to the attempt is what makes the actor's interpretation of a script dramatic, exciting, and clear. It is what makes an actor dynamic and bankable.

Another important point is that actors should not bring preconceived notions either to this old children's game or to acting itself. Because the game is so familiar, almost everyone will play it in the manner in which they played it as small children—adhering to all the rules they learned as first graders. Your students will likely play a fair and sober game, carefully following all those childhood rules.

Point out to your students the objective you initially stated: Get to "it" first, but if you are caught, you will be sent back to home base. The game, as presented, didn't call for integrity and fairness. Did your actors really have to adhere to boundaries not declared? Did they really have to go all the way back to home base if the game resumed before they got there? Did they really have to stop moving as soon as "it" called out "red light," or did they just assume they had to?

ROUND 3

Repeat the game, but this time make it clear that the objective is to win, not win according to a set of rules. The resulting game should be different.

DISCUSSION

This will be a much more exciting game to watch and to play. Many unexpected strategies will be used. Much more creativity will be displayed, and situations will arise that were not previously considered. Emphasize that this is not an exercise about cheating, but rather about the danger of making assumptions that are detrimental to exciting dramatic work. If everyone agrees that imaginative ways to win are appropriate and fair, then the conventional and obvious concepts about what is fair disappear. The unexpected becomes the norm. This makes for exciting acting.

Wrap-up

Once again the elements of risk and danger demonstrate to the student the parallels for its use in scripted material. Avoiding the mundane, the obvious, and the conventional, while still maintaining the rules of the game, can vastly improve a game of Red Light, Green Light. This is an equally important concept when doing scripted material. For example, how often does the young actor say good-bye and refuse to exit when doing scene work? The script shows more lines so the actor chooses to stay and say them. The actor has followed a preconceived notion that dialogue must mean a desire to stay and talk. However, if the acting objective really is to leave, the actor should leave. A new dramatic situation will result when the other actor in that scene is forced to detain the now departing actor. The same concept is true when applied to spoken dialogue. If the acting objective is to hurt or wound, for instance, that is what the actor should attempt to do, even if the scripted line says "I love you." Invariably the irony in the acted moment will be far more original, yet consistent with what is happening in the scene.

Actors must avoid preconceived notions and focus on their objectives. When they do, all the dramatic elements that surround them improve, and so does the work. Seeming to cheat when playing Red Light, Green Light can demonstrate this point and lead the student toward acting integrity.

The Gunfight

They stand in silence, not ten yards apart, their eyes locked together. Their features are invisible in the midday light—a pair of silhouettes frozen against the sun. Two percussive flashes in quick succession crack the stillness. Echoes panic up the alleyways and disappear into silence. The first shadowed figure, a dancer now, gracefully folds into the dusty street. An arm reaches up, strains, then collapses back into the dirt. A spur jingles as the lone upright silhouette saunters off. The prairie storm is over. This scene, played out a thousand times during my childhood on screens both large and small, is the inspiration for the fifth exercise in this chapter. In the previous exercises, we have been introduced to the concepts of conflict, story, objectives, throughlines, and physical action; of given circumstances, the "magic if," high stakes, and risk. But in the earlier exercises, actors were asked to create their stories in isolation. Now it is time to acknowledge and deal with another major dynamic that factors into the majority of acting work: Most acting onstage is necessarily a shared experience.

More often than not, acting situations are written as scenes played out between two characters on opposite sides of a dramatic conflict. Like a pair of tango dancers who intricately work together, interweaving moments in combination with moments of apposition, the twosome that make up the core of most acting situations must be totally connected with each other, even when their characters could not be further apart.

Actors must create and live in a shared world that is consistent for all involved. This is not as easy as it sounds. When an actor reads a scene or a play, a little movie forms in that actor's head. Another actor reading the same scene forms her own movie version. When those two actors come together to prepare that scene, they must give up their private little imaginary movies and create a new one together based on what they know about the scene as written and on what they pick up from each other as they develop the work. If they are unable to do this, their effort will most likely fail to be believable because their image is not a shared one. In addition, the work will probably lack spontaneity, the often surprising moment-to-moment reactions that can make the work truly exciting.

The best acting results when actors are listening to each other with all their senses, reacting at each moment to what their acting partners are giving them. This is what people do in life. All our senses give us information about what's going on in any situation. We instantaneously observe and analyze far more than the words being said. Unlike people in real life, however, actors must constantly be making choices that help them obtain their objectives so they can deliver the story it is their responsibility to tell. This balance between game plan and spontaneity is an essential part of the acting equation.

A typical Western gunfight provides the playing field for demonstrating all the above. The two actors are involved in a deadly conflict, one in which their objectives are all too clear. A set of given circumstances have brought these characters to this climactic high-risk situation, and the stakes could not be higher. Who does what when becomes critically important to how the story unfolds and to its ultimate outcome. Who does what when is also critically important to an audience's perception and reaction to that outcome. In other words, the way the gunfight plays out in conjunction with the information an audience gets along the way determines how the audience perceives the story and whether it finds the story effective and satisfying. For a theatrical presentation to be effective, it is essential that the actors are telling the same story that the audience sees. Both actors must study each other closely at all times and be totally interconnected at every moment. The Gunfight offers the beginning actor a serious challenge to his limited resources and shows him how difficult it is to make a seemingly simple scene work well.

Purpose

This exercise further develops the ability to use story, conflict, and objectives, to think in terms of throughlines of action, and to create a series of physical actions based on an understanding of the given circumstances, the "magic if," high stakes, and risk. The acting pairs will also have to develop their ability to work and react together moment by moment to make their stories not only believable, but exciting to watch. In addition, your students will learn that what an audience sees is not necessarily what the performers think an audience is seeing. They will begin appreciate the importance of building acting choices in such a way that they successfully communicate their intentions to an audience.

Method

Round 1

For the first round, divide your class into pairs. Ask them to stand, facing each other at about a distance of ten feet, if possible. When they are silently facing each other, ask them to look directly into their partner's eyes. Then tell them they are about to have a Western gunfight. Say to them, "Each of you has a revolver in your holster. Whenever you are ready, draw it from the holster and fire at your acting partner. Make the action as real as you can." That's all you need tell them for this first attempt. Let them go, and see what happens.

DISCUSSION

Believe it or not, from the very first moment, most of your actors will probably not be able to look at each other without laughing. The mere thought of themselves as gunfighters will drive many of them to hysterics. Other than playing off each other's laughter, they will be totally unconnected with each other and, for that matter, with the given circumstances of the exercise. They will demonstrate a total lack of concentration. There are many reasons for this. Asking your students to shoot at each other without props and then drop dead may be too much for them. Some will probably feel a bit naked; others downright silly. For most of them, being a cowboy is a very big jump. But as earlier exercises, such as Time Bomb, have demonstrated, concentration and commitment are essential ingredients if any acting task is to be successful.

Allow the laughter to run its course before retaking control of the situation. No point in trying to get serious before your students are ready and able, but once calm has settled in, talk about the need for concentration. Suggest that by focusing on the given circumstances and stakes of the situation, they can take themselves out of their own self-consciousness. The focus for the actor must always be outward. Actors must think about what they need (their objective) and go after it. That need, certainly while a character is involved in a high-stakes conflict with another character, cannot be internal. If your students think about their objective—in this case to win the gunfight so they will not die—they cannot feel silly.

Mastering the concentration necessary to look at each other as characters may take some time, and a few pairs may be too self-indulgent. Use your judgment to decide when patience should be replaced with a sterner approach. Certainly, by the time several pairs have successfully completed a gunfight, you should be pressing the rest to get onboard. Seeing those around them completing the assigned activity should help pull along the stragglers.

When each of your gunfight pairs have gotten through the exercise the first time, it will be time to discuss what you have seen. In all likelihood, it will not be a pretty picture. Much of what is lacking will be so obvious that you can critique the work in general by soliciting your students to comment on what they themselves did and what they saw. Their comments will probably include the following:

We didn't take each other seriously.

We laughed through the whole thing.

Who was shot was not clear.

There was a delayed reaction between the time of shooting and being shot.

No one dropped to the floor after being shot.

We both dropped to the floor at the same time.

It all happened so fast that nothing was clear.

There was no story.

When the shots fired, I didn't hear them so I didn't react.

Who shot whom, anyway?

The sequence from drawing the gun to firing it did not happen; it was all fake, it was just mush.

How am I supposed to fire a gun when I don't even know how to do it?

How do I do any of this stuff, for that matter?

Who am I supposed to be, anyway?

I wasn't sure whether I was supposed to be dead or just wounded, so I didn't play either.

Am I supposed to be glad that I killed the other guy?

What am I supposed to do when I'm shot?

Am I the good guy or bad guy?

And many, many more.

That's a lot of stuff to handle, and your class will probably now realize that even the simplest acting task can require a lot of thought before spontaneous in-the-moment acting can be executed with the freedom and commitment necessary to make it all work. They might even begin to realize that structure often increases possibilities rather than limiting them. How often in life do we find ourselves unable to make a decision when we haven't narrowed down the choices? It is the same with acting. Setting parameters can have a freeing effect. Given circumstances—whether made up, as in this exercise, or taken from a script—give actors the freedom to create.

ROUND 2

What your students should know for sure at this point is that gunfighting is a very dramatic situation. The stakes are life and death. That, in and of itself, should make an interesting sequence dramatically. The challenge for them will be to take those ingredients and mix them into a story that is as clear and as compelling as it should be.

For this round, make sure that your students understand that a gunfight sequence is already a story waiting to be told. If done properly, it has a beginning, middle, and end and a strong central conflict. Once this fact is clearly established, ask your gunfighting pairs to take a moment to talk to each other about the story they will be telling. This discussion should include the who, what, when, and where of the situation—the given circumstances surrounding the action. For this time through, remind your students to narrow their thinking down to the bare essentials that will make this sequence of actions work. Suggest that they make decisions on the basic elements of the story they are telling and to think about how they can best communicate those important elements to an audience. Remind them of the definition of good acting: Acting that is believable and that tells the best possible story. When they have outlined their story and given circumstances and feel they have made appropriate and effective choices to play out, let them proceed as in the first round.

DISCUSSION

When your gunfighters have completed their showdown, discuss what they saw and did as in the previous round. The gunfights this time should be far better and the necessary commitment will be much more in evidence. Now that your actors realize that the exercise is not going to go away, they will be taking it more seriously, and most of them will be able to execute their actions without laughing and with far less editorial commentary. They will have made some choices that help point out the necessary sequence of action.

For instance, if your actors have made even the most rudimentary decision about *who* they are, already the sequence of actions will have begun to take shape and, as a result, so will the shape of the story. Many of your student pairs will have decided who is the good guy and who is the bad guy in their situation. You can't get more simplistic than that, but this basic decision will automatically put them onto a sequence of choices that will enable them to tell a clearer and more interesting story. Will the bad guy draw first? If so, will his aim be true? Is the good guy quicker, or more accurate? If the bad guy guns down the good guy, what then? If the good guy triumphs over evil, how does he respond to the man he shot? If the bad guy is still standing, how does he react? Does he simply twirl his bad-guy moustache, or is his reaction more complex and sophisticated? Which is the better choice?

A few of your gunfighting actors might touch on the *what* of the story as well. The basic situation that has brought these two characters to center stage might provide some interesting groundwork for the choices possible in building this story. In other words, how do these two whos end up in this situation?

What is their relationship? How do they come to be standing on the street opposing each other? What is their experience, skill level, and attitude toward gunfighting? Most important, what is each thinking and feeling at this moment? These questions, and scores more, can add dimension and specificity to the choices you are asking your students to consider and make. But they will only do so if your students are able to translate these given circumstances into actions that reveal those circumstances to the audience.

Here's a possible scenario: The marshal is no gunfighter. He knows he is outclassed by his adversary. As he stands in the street, eye to eye with his potential killer, he knows he may be breathing his last breaths. How does the actor demonstrate this through his actions? The bad guy enjoys putting the marshal through this endgame torture because it is fun, because he knows he will win. The longer he can play out this torture the more pleasurable. What choices do your actors make to demonstrate this? Or, how about this: One of the gunfighters is a kid. He has never strapped on a gun before. His big mouth has gotten him into trouble. He is scared to death. His adversary must carry out the gunfight on a point of pride. He is skilled and knows he will easily triumph. He would much prefer to be playing poker in the saloon. Either of these scenarios can be supported and made clear through a series of well-chosen actions. Each can help make the scene specific and very interesting to play out and watch.

But, even if your students have done an excellent job defining their specific stories and have come up with choices that help them make their stories clear, their scene might still fail to work. This is where the listening and reacting part of acting craft comes into play. Each pair must be seeing each moment clearly and in a unified manner and reacting to it if the story is to be effectively rendered. If each actor is making and executing choices without connecting them to what her partner is doing, clarity and believability will not be possible.

Here are some examples of what I mean. The manner in which the first gunfighter draws his gun and fires must be clearly seen by the second gunfighter, who, in turn, must react in a specific and appropriate manner. This is essential if an audience is to believe the sequence and if the actors are to believably move on to the next sequence. Guns make sound and bullets fly on the trajectory in which they are aimed. The gunfighters must hear and see these actions and respond in an appropriate manner. A gun clearly aimed at a chest cannot believably produce a bullet hole in a leg, but it will in one or more of the scenes you witness. When a gunfighter falls to the ground, the manner in which he does so can and will affect his adversary. The actor watching his fall must observe closely and react with specificity. All actions and reactions must be timed out and reacted to in accordance with the way they were done in the moment—whether the moment was rehearsed or spontaneous. For many young performers not used to working with and off others, this aspect of the process is very difficult. No longer is acting simply about them alone.

Once again you will want to discuss what your actors saw and discovered during the second round. Besides what I have mentioned above, the sound of gunfire will probably be a big issue. Guns make a lot of noise, and the percussive nature of gunfire is an automatic attention galvanizer in real life, but without that sound in your students' gunfights, many of your actors may get tripped up. Some might make their own gun sounds, others might not acknowledge sound at all. One way or another, the fact remains that firing a gun does have a dramatic sound and that sound must be accounted for in the work. This issue will come up again in the next round.

By the time your post–Round 2 discussion is over, your actors will probably realize that the choices they make must be not only analyzed and selected but also be made believable and tangible through the rehearsal process. Your actors will have learned that it is not the back story (all that happened prior to what the audience sees) that needs to be told during the gunfight. Rather, it is the choices they make in the present, inspired by the back story they created together. Asking the right questions and coming up with effective answers is a cornerstone to building an acting technique or craft that is both reliable and exciting. Your students will also realize that to effectively accommodate all that must occur in a gunfight, the R word—rehearsal—is essential. Learning to see and react in the moment seldom just happens. Now you've got them where you want them: They know that the R word is good.

ROUND 3

This will be a rehearsal round, but before you send your students off to rehearse, or give them The Gunfight as a prepared assignment, add a few new thoughts to the mixture. Ask your class where the big moments of the scene are (the moments that hold the most dramatic stuff). Have them define the throughline of action by pointing out where those dramatic stepping-stone moments actually occur. Suggest through your discussion that by defining these moments they are actually shaping the story they will be telling.

Ask your students to write a scenario describing the action of the scene they will rehearse. Included in this paragraph should be the given circumstances and a step-by-step description of the action—the things that actually happen in the scene. You will probably want to give this as an overnight homework assignment or as an assignment due at the end of class. After you approve the written scenario, allow a significant amount of time—a full class period or another overnight assignment—for preparation.

When the gunfight scenes are ready for presentation, each pair should perform their rehearsed work with little introductory explanation. The intent here is to encourage your students to bring as much clarity to the work on their own as they can so that additional explanation becomes unnecessary. When each presentation is finished, the class will discuss what they have seen. The discussion should focus on what parts of the scene worked and what didn't. If possible, each scene should be reworked after the discussion (either as an assignment or during assigned class time) so that each pair of actors has an opportunity to incorporate any useful suggestions and to rework any elements that fell short the first time through.

DISCUSSION

The presentation by your students of their prepared scenes is the "High Noon" of their acting work thus far. They will have incorporated all the concepts and obligations of previous work, but this time they will have rehearsed together, working toward the presentation of a story that is clear and exciting; one that seems as real and spontaneous as life itself. In addition, this time an audience will be watching—an audience willing to go with the unfolding story but not willing to fill in details left unclear or left out altogether or to trust an unbelievable situation.

Some of your student critics will be too kind. Their desire to receive a gentle critique during their own performance will compromise their commentary. This attitude should be discouraged. Honest feedback helps an actor grow.

Much of the feedback will be usefully honest and accurate, however, and this critique may shock the performers. They might argue that their critics do not know what they are talking about. This, of course, is not productive. The audience is the final arbiter of what works and what does not, and an actor develops her craft ultimately for an audience's eyes. Your job will be to sift the commentary for its core truth, to separate and point out which comments are on target and which are not, to explain the difference between nitpicky and important, and to make your actors understand that they must be receptive to criticism—for only when they are, will they grow. The best way for your actors to learn their craft is by actively watching others work. By analyzing why something they see onstage works or why it doesn't, actors develop skills that can be applied to their own work.

A common complaint from students is the lack of audible gunfire. It will be difficult in some cases for the audience to believe and understand the moment of gunfire without sound. It will also be difficult for the actors to clearly recognize those moments as well, because the actual sound is the clearest marker for that occurrence. Acting teams that create their own sound for gunfire will generally be more successful in those moments. The sound of artificial gunfire will probably be the topic of an interesting discussion because your class will likely come to the realization that even a silly, kidlike, manufactured sound is better than no sound at all. All those gunfire noises that your students made as kids will be tested in their scenes. What your students will discover is that as long as there is consistency in the artificial sound, the audience will suspend their disbelief. This, of course, is one cornerstone of theatrical presentation.

LATER ROUNDS

Hopefully, after the discussion of each scene is completed, your students can rehearse their scenes again, this time incorporating as many useful comments as they can. After all, it is by working and reworking material that a polished piece of acting is produced. It is also part of the necessary discipline that all artists must learn to accept and relish. New choices will lead, of course, to new and better work and to new problems for the audience as well. You will need to encourage your students to accept that continuous trial and error is part of the acting process.

Another round of the exercise might include several variations. You could allow a line or two of dialogue at the beginning and end of the scene, or perhaps one line at the beginning and one at the end, giving each character a single line. You could provide your actors with the lines, or they could write the lines themselves. Remind them that the lines should contribute directly to the story.

You might try variations on The Gunfight. Suppose this is a formal duel rather than a showdown? Note the changes in given circumstances and characterization this would require. Or ask your partners to change roles, yet do the same things. How recasting changes the story can lead to a productive discussion on what an actor brings to a role.

Wrap-up

The Gunfight requires actors to do all the things they will be expected to do when bringing a script to life. But, most important, it makes clear that acting is not about solo performing. In the best acting, actors share a moment and simultaneously react to it together and independently. Experiencing that connective link shows your young actors what they should strive for—the ability to both serve a script and excite an audience.

Using Physical Actions

In the previous chapter, I described a series of games intended to introduce basic acting concepts that included playing objectives fully, the use of conflict and high stakes, the importance of listening, and the value of making strong, dramatic choices. Mastery of these concepts leads to solid acting—acting that is believable and that tells the most exciting story possible.

Actors are, after all, the medium through which the good story is told. The playwright, the director, and the audience all rely on the actors to move the plot forward as well as to reveal the inner workings of the characters they are playing. This must be done with imagination, clarity, and simplicity if the play is to work. It must be accomplished in a logical, step-by-step sequence if the story of the play is to unfold with dramatic precision.

Aside from dialogue, actors' physical actions are the cornerstone of any performance, for it is only through what actors say and do that their characters and stories are revealed. It is essential that actors know the given circumstances of any acting situation. They must know what their characters' needs are at any given moment, but without dialogue it is only through the actors' specific physical choices that these circumstances, thoughts, and needs are communicated to an audience.

Actors, especially student actors, spend an inordinate amount of time being concerned with what their characters are feeling rather than with what their characters are doing. All too often this preoccupation ends up complicating and obfuscating what the playwright has worked so hard to make clear—namely the story. If actors find ways to make the story that is unfolding physical, without clouding it up with unnecessary emotion and action, their work will be clear and interesting, and the story will get told. Here are two exercises that can help make the point for clear, direct acting. Each exercise relies on physical actions that can be done clearly and simply.

An Almost Silent Story

Purpose
To demonstrate that when actors carry out a step-by-step, logical sequence of actions that have beginnings, middles, and ends, their work will not only be clear, exciting, and repeatable but will also carry with it all the requisite emotion for them to express and the audience to observe.

Method
The description that follows should be read aloud by the teacher while each actor executes the actions being described. This exercise has the best results when it is done using one actor at a time, but several actors could, if necessary, work simultaneously. Please note the following to your class before reading:

It will be necessary to repeat an action several times because each new piece of information colors and/or changes what has already been read and performed.

All actions must be executed fully.

Each action should have a beginning, middle, and end.

Each action should be accomplished in a manner that specifically reflects the given circumstances explained, suggested, or implied by the material.

Getting it right the first time is not important; making and exploring choices to find things that work, and work well, is.

Each new action should logically follow the preceding one.

It is the actor's job to make the transition from one action to another clearly and logically.

It is the teacher's job to point out when that is not happening.

A character enters her living room from the front door after cutting the lawn on a hot summer afternoon. She notices that the living room is stifling. She realizes that the window air conditioner is not on. She goes to the far end of the room where the air conditioner is located. She tries to turn it on. She cannot. She notices that it is unplugged and reaches for the cord. She plugs it in and tries to turn on the air conditioner again. She cannot. She looks around the room and notices the table by the door. She goes to the table, opens the drawer in the front, and rummages through it until she finds something. It is a screwdriver. She closes the drawer and returns to the window with the tool. She sticks the screwdriver into the air conditioner's control panel and turns something with difficulty. She stops. She begins again, this time struggling to turn something. She stops. She puts down the screwdriver. She presses a button on the control panel. She bangs the air conditioner with her fist. She turns and looks around the room. She returns to the table. She opens the drawer again and rummages through it. She finds something. It is a hammer. She closes the drawer. She returns to the air conditioner. She bangs the control panel gently. She waits. She bangs the control panel again. She presses the button on the control panel. She puts her hands out in front of her. She lifts her face toward the air conditioner. She steps in front of it completely. The character fans the cool air against her. She withdraws her head. She looks around the room. She goes to a chair and sits. She takes off her sneakers one at a time. She sits back in her chair. The phone rings. She gets up and crosses to the phone on the wall. She picks up the receiver and says, "Hello." She listens for some time and finally says, "Good-bye." She hangs up the phone. She returns to her chair. She sits. She puts her head in her hands and does not look up again.

DISCUSSION

Because so much of the physical action (the things that the character actually does) in this exercise is clearly laid out, the acting task is relatively simple. In the places where the description specifically says what to do, you should make sure your actors are doing the actions specifically and completely. Each action should start with the impulse or reason for doing it—that is the real beginning to any action.

Every action your actors execute must demonstrate purpose or, in acting terms, objective. If the character is hot, for instance, then the specific purpose of her walk to the air conditioner is to turn it on so she can get relief from the heat. How important is it to get relief? It is always a better choice to make the need great. The walk to the air conditioner should demonstrate this fact. This same principle should apply to all other physical actions—sitting, getting the screwdriver, going to the phone.

There are other times in the exercise where action is implied, but not stated directly. For instance, the discovery that the room is hot requires a physical action to demonstrate the discovery. You can help your actors explore a variety of choices. You and the class, by responding as the audience, can help the working actor decide which choices work best, that is, which ones are the most clear and the most interesting. The same process applies to feeling the cool breeze blowing from the air conditioner, moving, and standing in front of it, discovering the sensation of feet released from their shoe prison, and the reaction to sitting back in the chair. Each of these feelings requires some physical action that demonstrates clearly how the completed action feels.

Imagining the feeling is not enough if the actor is to communicate her feeling clearly to the audience.

It is worth mentioning here that some actors may not be able to feel the sensations at all. But as that song from *A Chorus Line* suggests, "feeling nothing" does not necessarily mean failure. If the audience thinks the character felt something, then your actors have done their job. A solid physical action can create the impression that the actor is thoroughly invested in the feeling. On the other hand, a well-felt feeling that is not communicated to the audience is probably worthless. Actors must learn to work for the audience, not themselves—the trick is to make the audience think you felt it.

During the phone call part of the exercise, the actor's task becomes more difficult. She must listen and respond to the caller's words and find ways to suggest as clearly as possible what the content of the call actually is. Of course, the actor must first decide for herself, before any response can be chosen. Once she clearly knows the content, it is then her responsibility to make physical choices that communicate it to the audience. Obviously, if the actor makes the news dramatic, then she has more to react to, and her choice of physical actions can powerfully correspond to this set of circumstances.

The actor is obligated to say good-bye at the end of the phone conversation in a manner that reflects the news just received. The way she crosses back to the chair, sits again, and places her hands on her head must all reflect her choices concerning the phone call. As read, this series of physical actions strongly suggest a major dramatic moment, and you, as the teacher, should encourage your actors to explore the dramatic possibilities fully. A good actor will leave no action unexplored. How should the phone be hung up? What is the right tempo for the cross back to the chair? What is an appropriate pace for bringing the hands to the head? How long should that moment be held? These, and a hundred more questions, can provide the impetus for exploration and discovery.

Wrap-up

Beginning actors usually have the misconception that acting is about feeling, and that if they are able to feel fully, they are doing their job as actors. This dangerous misconception usually leads to "emoting" in the worst possible sense and often results in acting that goes nowhere. On the other hand, well-thought-out, believable physical actions can provide a reliable conduit to emotional truth. The same can seldom be said of a conjured emotion.

All humans have the capacity for pretend. When we play games, we commit to them as if they are real. Victories and defeats can be as meaningful in a game as in life. When we are chased in a game of tag, for instance, we play our objective—running away so that we don't get caught—fully and with commitment. We pretend that not getting tagged is important, and we come to believe it is so. As "it" begins to catch up to us, we feel fear, real and palpable. Are we acting?

This same phenomenon will happen in acting when actors commit to choices as they would commit to a game. Well-chosen physical actions are the actor's game of tag. For instance, when the actor is supposed to be angry in a scene, he might kick a chair. Once he begins to kick it, he often begins to feel angry. But even if he doesn't, kicking the chair demonstrates his anger clearly to the audience. Usually, however, a well-chosen and reliable physical action causes the actor to feel the very thing he is trying to communicate.

Physical actions are tangible, repeatable, and controllable. They allow the actor to tell the story in terms that an audience can understand. They often lead to the very emotions actors try so hard to conjure without action. This is one of the biggest lessons that An Almost Silent Story demonstrates.

Add an Action

Purpose

As in An Almost Silent Story, this exercise gets the student actor to use physical actions to tell a story. Your students have already learned that a story must have a conflict of some kind and must build dramatically. They have probably also learned by now that each moment tells a story if it is specifically and clearly executed. An Almost Silent Story demonstrates and reinforces that a sequence of well-executed physical actions can generate feeling in the actor and help him communicate those feelings clearly to an audience.

Method

The game is simple to play. The first actor steps up onto the stage, or into the center of the circle of actors, and executes a single, complete physical action. This physical action should have a beginning, middle, and end. For instance, the first actor enters the space and stops. The next actor repeats the first action and adds a new action that follows logically from the first; that actor might turn his head to the left and to the right. As each new actor takes a turn, the additional actions should develop a story that is simple, clear, logical, and, hopefully, dramatically interesting. The exercise is over when all actors have had a chance to contribute an action, or whenever the story has been completed, or when you, as coach, think it is.

Here is an example of how the game might proceed. The third actor repeats the first two actions—the entrance, the stop, the head turn. He now walks several steps forward and stops. The next actor might add a 90-degree turn to the left. The fourth might throw up her hands in front of her face. The fifth might fall to the ground, or slowly lower his hands from his face.

The sequence I have just described could represent the actions of a character who almost got hit by a car. The physical actions themselves, although properly sequenced, do not tell the story. However, if your actors execute the actions in a manner appropriate to the situation, that situation will become clear. The manner of walking, looking, stepping into the street, and turning toward the oncoming automobile will all contribute to the clarity of the sequence. Really looking both ways, really hearing the oncoming car, really turning toward the squealing tires will provide your actors with solid acting opportunities.

DISCUSSION

Getting your students to perform a complete, single physical action is probably the most difficult aspect of the game. Often, you will find that, because students are not absolutely clear about what they are doing, they improvise while they are working. This invariably leads to several shadow actions rather than one single, completed action. The net result will be a lack of clarity in the choice and its execution, or a sequence of actions too vague or numerous to remember. Don't allow this to happen. Keep your students honest by forcing them to create and execute a single, clear action. This will help develop in your students an appreciation for clarity in their work. As they attempt to maintain a story line while they follow each other in sequence, the vagueness or specificity of the preceding work will become eminently clear. Only when the previous action is understood can the next actor add an action that makes sequential sense. Only if audience members can understand what is happening from moment to moment can they follow the flow of a story onstage.

All storytelling requires beginnings, middles, and ends. This is true for physical actions as with any other aspects of acting. All physical choices start with the impulse to do the action. Ensure your actors make those moments of decision physical. They are actable and must be delivered clearly. An audience will never understand why an actor does what he does if that clarity is missing. These acting moments usually occur during *transitions*—when an actor abandons something old for something new. They are usually moments when objectives are completed through victories or defeats, when new ideas come to mind, when discoveries are made, when actions are interrupted, or when new information is introduced.

Do not let your students make illogical or nondramatic additions. It is your job to make sure that each new action propels the story forward, to condition them to sense what is dramatically interesting, and to get them to realize that they are the storytellers. It is up to them to create as well as execute choices that are logical, clear, and exciting.

Wrap-up

Add an Action can be played over and over again. Its plot possibilities are virtually infinite. Comedy and drama can each be explored and developed, even by using identical sequences of action. At times it might be beneficial for you to start the game yourself. That way you can influence or control how the game will unfold. You might want to consider in advance what beginning physical actions to introduce. You might even come in with an entire sequence of physical actions to ensure the game takes off in the direction you want it to. It is even possible to introduce the concept of style while playing this game. What would happen if you told your students to execute their action in classical Greek fashion or in Elizabethan style? Suppose you told them to create a farce? Don't forget to consider and manipulate given circumstances such as time and place. Get your students thinking as actors. There is no limit to the possibilities. Use your own creativity.

Regardless of the style your students portray, the most important lessons in this exercise result from the moment-to-moment work forced on them. Each added action requires a decision about the previous one, and each new decision must be demonstrated to the audience. When actors share their thought processes through their physical actions, they not only compel audience members to watch them, but they also irresistibly invite them to empathize and engage. What more could a storyteller ask for?

Scenes from the Shower

In the two previous games, student actors learned to think in terms of physical actions—physical choices that communicate to an audience what a character is thinking, feeling, and doing at any particular moment. When these actions are executed clearly and simply with conviction, the story of the character in the moment, in the beat, or in the entire play is magically brought to life with minimal ambiguity.

In the following two exercises, the concept of story for the actor will be further developed. All acting requires an awareness of story, and the actor must strive to tell the best story he can at every moment onstage. The trick, however, is that the actor must never tell his own story at the expense of the overall story of the script, and the actor must never make choices that violate the logic of the situation or character. The actor must always serve the play.

By definition, story entails plot, character, and setting. At the center of every plot exists one or more conflicts that move characters into opposition. This plot, with a beginning, middle, and end, rises to a climax and then falls again. If actors remember that they are telling stories at every moment, then it follows that they will strive to find conflict at all times, ensuring that the story continues to be interesting. It is all too easy, however, to go off track as actors respond to the stimulation of the moment. The trained actor has learned to make the choices that offer the most dramatic possibilities while at the same time make logical sense in the moment. This is the point of the exercises that follow.

The Solo Shower

Purpose

This exercise demonstrates that acting requires good storytelling as well as believability. It is not enough just to be real. Good acting, as well as a good play, require an organization of events and actions that give the work heightened meaning.

Method

Have your student actors take a shower in front of the class. This can be done as a prepared assignment or as an in-class improvisation. A prepared assignment is better, but time restraints may prevent that. Tell your students that each shower action must be done in the proper sequence and that the execution of each action must be so specific as to be indistinguishable from reality. If the exercise is a prepared assignment, then the standard for judgment should be higher. Do not allow students to use props. Imagination, specificity, and rehearsal can and should make clear what the props might have accomplished. Props and their use are not to be scorned. They can and should make the actor's task more easy. However, the struggle for specifics in choice and execution is one of the purposes of this exercise. (By the way, The Solo Shower should be taken fully clothed. It may be ill-advised to allow your students to take off their clothes, no matter how insistent they are. You could end up in trouble, and they could catch cold. Even worse, they may lose their focus!)

Discussion

The good student actor will no doubt bring in a well-thought-out and rehearsed exercise. The work will certainly include great attention to sensory detail with physical actions that have beginnings, middles, and ends. When the actor reaches for the soap, the audience will believe that she is doing so because the actor sees and feels that soap in her mind's eye. The actor will establish the need for the soap before reaching for it because she knows that actions require motivation, and audiences are better served when they can see that motivation. The well-rehearsed exercise will move from one physical action to another in a logical sequence that has continuity and clarity. The exercise will not simply end; it will have finished.

However, even when the exercise is perfectly accomplished, an extremely important element in the good actor's thinking process has been so far ignored. The exercise, as described and executed, has been too general and has had no specific dramatic content. Plays are not written about the commonplace, the mundane. Good plays are always written about the extraordinary. Marsha Norman's *'night Mother* is not about all the boring, repetitive days of her main character, Jesse. It is about one particular night, the night she has decided to kill herself. Hamlet does not concern itself with the young prince's banal days at school, but rather it begins on a night when the ghost of Hamlet's father is walking the ramparts.

Actors are storytellers much like the dramatist. It is up to the actor to tell the best story she possibly can at all times. A believably imagined and executed shower is no small feat. But a believable shower that is dramatically compelling is a far better shower to take and to watch. So, the student actor should have asked herself a series of questions before rehearsing her shower exercise. The answers to her questions would have provided her with a compelling dramatic structure that would have greatly enhanced the exercise.

Dramatic structure always starts with conflict. When using a script it is up to the actor to discover the dramatic conflict contained within its pages. When the actor is her own playwright, then it is up to her to provide the detail. This discipline will always enhance any piece of work an actor does. Perhaps the conflict involves time. The shower taker is late. What is she late for? Breakfast? Work? An important meeting with the boss? The job interview of her life? Which provides her with the best storytelling opportunities? That is the one she should choose. It will give her the most to do, even in the context of shower taking.

If the character is in a rush, for instance, all the actions she has rehearsed now take on a heightened meaning. Everything from reaching for the soap to adjusting the water temperature becomes more difficult—obstacles for the actor to overcome in order to reach her goal of making her interview on time.

Every given circumstance that the actor makes up for herself can and should contribute to the dramatic conflict. Suppose it is cold out? Suppose the water pressure is bad, or the hot and cold balance keeps changing? Suppose the soap is slippery?

Suppose shampoo gets in her eyes? Suppose she can't reach the towel? Each of these ideas could enhance the situation, or make the ordinary extraordinary, without destroying believability. There are, of course, an infinite number of reasons to be taking a shower. It is up to the actor/storyteller to choose a compelling one.

Once the actor knows the specific given circumstances (who he is, where he is, when the story is occurring), then it is his responsibility to find and execute the physical actions appropriate to the situation. What if the character had just been molested? What if the shower follows a football player's triumph or defeat? Suppose it is a little girl's first shower by herself? Suppose the character hates to shower, never takes them, but is a guest at someone's house? An actor must be his own playwright. Without a context, choices will reflect the ordinary. This is no crime, but the actors who get hired most often are the ones that bring excitement along with believability. Which kind of actor should you be training?

Wrap-up

The possibilities in situational choices and in the execution of actions are infinite. But the more specific the given circumstances, the more specific the choices can be. Even if your students keep the same sequence of physical actions time after time, by shifting any or all the given circumstances, the story line and its execution will continue to change. Remember, the purpose of the exercise is to tell the best story possible. Your students should be encouraged to keep searching for that story.

The Group Shower

Purpose

The purpose of this exercise is to expose the student actor to the concept of Stanislavski's "magic if" and to get them thinking with logical choices that focus on the most important and interesting elements of an unfolding story.

Method

Tell your students that they will be doing a group improvisation. Tell them they have found themselves together, away from civilization, in a cabin with one large community shower space with several shower heads. There is no place to hide. Tell them that when the exercise begins, they must quickly shower and dress. Make time an important element so they will not avoid getting into the shower for too long. Begin the exercise and see what happens.

DISCUSSION

This improvisation is intended to be a stop-and-go exercise in which your observation and coaching is a critical element. The acting concepts you will probably spend the most time on include the following: logical sequence (Does one action follow logically from the previous one?), objective and focus (Do the actors play objectives that are consistent with what is most important in the moment?), justification (Are the actions that occur supported by the given circumstances established?), and the "magic if" (If I were the character in this situation, how would I behave?).

To some extent this exercise is a trick, especially if you do it following extensive work on The Solo Shower exercise. After focusing so hard on making a story out of the ordinary ingredients of shower taking, most of your student actors will probably focus on their showering process rather than the big dramatic element of the situation—the fact that they're all standing around together naked. Start the exercise and let it go on for a while. When you stop to discuss, eventually ask why so many of them ignored the fact that they are seeing each other naked for the first time. Many will probably rationalize their explanation, but just keep hitting them with the "magic if." Each time your actors redo the exercise, more of them will deal with the nudity issue, and they will find that this provides a much better springboard for a story than any of their rationalized justifications for focus. The obvious situational ingredient—they are all naked—is clearly the most interesting story element for the actors and for the audience. Once your students acknowledge the nudity in the situation, they will easily find a strong objective to play.

Beginnings, middles, and ends also play an important part in this exercise. The dramatic action, for instance, does not begin with the nudity; it really begins when the characters realize they have to get naked in front of the others. How will these characters react? Will they be shocked, mortified, delighted, curious, proud? All these choices are possible, but the choice must begin with the discovery of the situation. That is a playable moment, and the actors will have to decide who their characters are and what attitudes they possess before they can play their actions. It will be up to your actors to convert these emotions into physical actions that can be seen by the audience, motivated by objectives that they can commit to and try to attain.

Early on in the exercise your actors will probably start asking questions, sometimes very smart questions. For instance, they might ask why this group of people would be willing to get undressed in front of the others. It is up to you to help your students come up with given circumstances that might justify this action. Be inventive, but try not to totally violate reality. Perhaps the group is on an Outward Bound adventure, or perhaps the group is a recalcitrant bunch forced to "rough it" as a court-mandated disciplinary measure. If you get desperate, you could just say "because that's the way it is." Ridiculous as the situation might seem, it is no more ridiculous than the situation that often confronts the actor when doing an absurdist play. It is a valid acting exercise to deal with the given circumstances in a believable manner no matter how ridiculous they might appear. As the work proceeds, your actors should be encouraged to discover playable moments that are repeatable. By building their own throughlines, one moment at a time, a nice story line for the exercise can be quickly developed, especially if the individual work is supported with clearly chosen physical actions and objectives. Your students will soon begin to sense how their individual stories contribute to the whole without making their own work dominate at every moment. They will begin to sense how the big story is better served when their own stories serve rather control the big picture.

When I do this exercise with my own students, the characters they first develop are almost always their own age. Therefore, their acting choices reflect their own kinds of behavior to a major degree. At some point you might want to have your students play characters of a different age in this same situation. This means they will have to re-justify the given circumstances for the age and group selected, but this won't be so hard now that the improvisation has been firmly established. For instance, how might middle-aged people respond in a group shower situation? How might old people? A group of clergy? Hippies? Ten-year-olds? Explore with your students. Just make sure the choices they make are specific, consistent for their characters, justified, logical, and, of course, interesting.

Wrap-up

What need would bring an older person into a situation like this? What would motivate a middle-aged woman to undress in front of strangers? The Group Shower exercise can help open up the door for thought and analysis about a whole range of people and values that might not normally occur to a group of young students. The educational opportunities are literally infinite. With all these available possibilities, many broader educational purposes can and should be served. Of course, there are the specific acting benefits it can afford your students as well. Now, who says that acting serves no broader educational purposes? So go ahead. Jump in. And don't forget your towel!

Pictures at an Exhibition

Several years ago at the Museum of Modern Art in New York City, I had the pleasure of attending the Picasso Exhibition, one of the great art shows of our time. It was also one of the most popular, drawing crowds similar to those found outside Space Mountain at Disney World. Picasso's paintings, not unlike the offerings at Mickeyland, have become pop culture icons that can draw huge crowds with a vast demographic spread. Highbrows, lowbrows, and even nobrows all pushed and jostled their way into the museum to see the works of one of the most famous artists in Western culture. The crowds were so great, it was impossible to really look at the works. I had to return several times to see the exhibit, often going early or late to avoid the crowds.

Once I discovered those off-peak times for viewing the exhibition, I found I could more carefully observe not only the artwork but the people viewing the artwork. I discovered that, for me, the viewers were almost as interesting to look at and often more easy to understand and appreciate than the art they were perusing. Since, for many, Picasso is an acquired taste, requiring a knowledge of what he was trying to do with his work, the range of reactions that people demonstrated with their bodies was fascinating and often hilarious. At times I was reminded of the Hans Christian Andersen fairy tale about the emperor's new clothes. Like the subjects who were afraid to offend their monarch, an enormous number of people looked at Picasso's paintings pretending to understand and appreciate what their body language clearly suggested they did not. At other times, they clearly demonstrated their puzzlement, lack of empathy, and even disdain. From my viewing bench, I was able to follow the stories of many museum-goers from the moment they approached a particular piece until they left the gallery room. While watching their sequence of behaviors and trying to determine their thoughts through the actions they unconsciously completed, the seeds for this exercise were planted.

Purpose

This exercise introduces or reminds acting students of their responsibilities as actors to their script and to their audience while giving them the opportunity to employ the basic tools of their craft. If they do a good job with the exercise, they will be not only be believable, they will also tell an interesting story that is clear and compelling. To do so, they will need to create a dramatic structure to their sequence of actions. They will need to create given circumstances, conflict, and physical actions with beginnings, middles, and ends. They will need to play strong objectives, make clear transitions, and create a throughline. That about covers the basics of what actors do with any script.

Method

Ask the members of your class to act out the following situation: They enter a museum and look at three paintings from an exhibition. It is probably best if the exhibition shows the work of a single artist. There should be no dialogue, and any interaction between the actors onstage (if you choose to have them work at the same time) should be the interaction of strangers. It is probably better not to have your entire class work at the same time because the audience's response is an important component of the exercise. (If you are the only one watching, then you must do all the commentary.) You can have your actors enter in groups, or you can stagger their entrances in some other way. An effective method is to have half your class observe the other half, discuss what was seen, and reverse positions. If you have the time, you can let each student do the exercise individually. As your student audience begins gathering observations, try to get them to establish what works and what does not. Usually, they come to agree that acting that is clear and believable and creates an interesting story works best.

I usually have my students do this exercise at least twice. The first time they do it, it is without preparation and rehearsal. I give them only a few minutes to think about what they will do and to make some preliminary choices. The discussion that follows the completion of the exercise provides them with some hints about the preparation they will need to do for Round 2. The second time through will be a fully prepared and rehearsed exercise.

ROUND 1

The first round of the game is intended to demonstrate to your student actors the two sides of the acting equation. First, actors must be believable in what they do, to themselves if possible, but certainly to the audience. Second, and this is the half not always so obvious, they must also be responsible for making and carrying out choices that are not only interesting in and of themselves but also communicable to the audience. A great idea that an actor cannot make the audience understand and follow is not a great idea. Acting is done for an audience, period.

In the first round your students will be looking at pictures that the audience will have no way of seeing. They will move from one to the next, sometimes with no apparent reason; sometimes with a reason, but not with one the audience can fathom. In all probability, even if the actions are believable, your students will not compose a story that allows them to travel on a journey during their time onstage. A journey suggests plot and plot suggests action. People go to the theater and the movies to see a story. Work that contains an interesting story is more successful than work that does not.

On the positive side, your student audience will likely be most impressed by moments that are fully executed with clarity—moments that have clearly defined beginnings, middles, and ends. Student actors must learn that actions don't begin with the actions themselves; rather, they begin with the impulse for action. If the actor decides to move closer to the painting for a better look, she should make sure that this decision-making moment is played fully. This moment is as important as the move itself and as dramatically interesting. The "lightbulb" moment must be communicated. By the same token, when the actor decides to move from one painting to the next, the audience should understand why that action is taking place now rather than a few moments ago or a few moments from now. In life, people don't need to communicate their reasons for action, but onstage, the actor does.

DISCUSSION
During the discussion, your students should make a clear distinction between what they actually saw and what they believe they saw. The observing students should not do interpretive work. If the actors performing have not presented their story clearly and fully, then what they did was not effective. An audience is not responsible for deciphering cryptic stage actions. They should not be forced into doing the actor's job. I often tell my classes that I have trained myself to be the "dumbest person in the class." This ensures that my students make clear choices at every moment onstage.

Once the exercise has been performed by everyone and discussed for its successes and failures, for its clear and cloudy moments, for its specificity or lack thereof, the requirements for a successful exercise will probably have become clear. At that point, the exercise should be given as a homework assignment and be brought in fully thought-out and rehearsed by your students. Here is a partial list of things they will need to think about and present clearly.

Given Circumstances
Who. Who is the character the actor is playing? What is her attitude about art, about this artist specifically, and about the three particular paintings being observed? How can these choices be made clear to the audience? What are the paintings? Who is the artist? Why has the actor picked these paintings? This artist? Or more precisely, can these paintings and this artist be suggested by the selected physical actions of the artist?

When. What is the time of day? the season? the year? Do these choices help to tell a good story? How can they be used to tell a good story? How can they be conveyed clearly to the audience?

Where. What country, city, museum, wing of museum does the action take place in? What does the viewing room itself look like? How do the answers chosen help tell the story clearly and in an interesting manner?

Conflict and Objectives
What conflict can the actor build into her story to ensure that the work is interesting? Why is the character viewing the exhibition? A homework assignment? Love of art? Curiosity? The more specific the choice, the more specific and clear the character's actions and reactions will be to the audience.

Dramatic Structure
What sequence of actions happens to the character from the time she enters the space until she leaves? Is there a throughline? Does the character go through some changes during the exercise? Is the character different as a result of viewing these paintings? Where are the moments that suggest these changes to the audience? Does a plot unfold step-by-step, clearly and with a build?

Physical Actions
Do the actions that the actor chooses to execute actually and specifically make clear what is going on moment to moment? Do these actions have beginnings, middles, and ends? Are moments of transition identified and well-thought-out? Will they be executed physically in such a way that they will be clear to the audience?

ROUND 2
In Round 2, there are many traps that the actor can fall into. Most of them have to do with the choices they make with the given circumstances. Very often my own student actors will end up saying to me in frustration, "Well, how was I supposed to

do that? Why don't you show me how you would make that landscape by Turner clear?!" The answer is that I probably couldn't. But I also would have had the sense not to select a landscape by Turner, and that is the point. Hopefully, your students will make choices that they can execute and communicate clearly. This is an essential ingredient to any good acting work. If the actor is not capable of fulfilling her good idea onstage, then it is not an idea to keep on the table. Acting is about choices, and it is always a good choice to jettison what does not work. An actor must learn to be practical.

It is essential that your students pick an artist for whom they can make physical choices that will communicate who the artist is. If the artist can be recognized, that artist's most famous work will likely pop into the heads of the audience. Once the audience has a frame of reference, chances are a single, well-chosen, physical action will communicate the specific painting. What physical actions come to mind for Picasso, for Seurat, for Van Gogh? What could be done to suggest Jackson Pollack, Leonardo da Vinci, or El Greco?

Once the artist has been established, what three pieces of work should your students use? The selection should not be arbitrary. The three pieces will need to be arranged in a way that builds a dramatic progression. If the artist is Picasso, for instance, I might start with an early work, one that bears a relation to the reality I know. A doable sequence might start with *Harlequin*, move to an early cubist work, then perhaps end with that giant mural of murals, *Guernica*. Certainly, even if not understood, *Guernica* is impressive in size and scope. An actor could easily make choices that would demonstrate these qualities.

In a Van Gogh, the colors and texture of the works often dominate. What actions could suggest those characteristics? How might the colors and thickness of the paint draw in the viewer? What things might the viewer do to get a better look at the vibrancy, at the texture? How could the actor use space, angle, and distance to communicate these ideas? What three Van

Goghs could be communicated? How could they be arranged to tell the story of the viewer? How would the character traits of the viewer influence how she percieves the paintings by Van Gogh?

It is important to keep in mind that this is an exercise. Very few students will be successful in all aspects of this assignment. The point is to plant in their heads the idea that actors must think as well as react and behave, and that solid thinking can go a long way toward solving any acting problem. I have had students do a wonderful job telling the story of their characters even when I could not determine who the artists and paintings were. But the artists and paintings were very clear and specific to the performers. As a result, the actors were able to develop a through-line of action that clearly demonstrated the progressive impact the works of art had on them as characters. Because they had made such specific decisions for themselves, their stories were presented clearly and compellingly, even though the identities of the artists and their work were not.

In many of the more successful exercises I have seen, the common thread was the journey of discovery—the step-by-step road to understanding and then appreciation or scorn for what was being observed. It is a rule of thumb that the greater the distance the acting journey covers, the more interesting the story and the acting that makes it clear. If the character enters the museum not planning to like what she is about to see, and then, through a step-by-step process, discovers that she does, a foundation for a fine dramatic work has been provided. The specific moments of growing understanding and final judgment become the connective links of the story chain. Portraying these moments clearly and strongly will make both the actor and the exercise successful. By the same token if the actor enters the scene fully expecting to love what she is about to behold, then the trail of disappointment leading to disdain can provide an equally effective throughline. There are many other scenarios, of course, and the ones that provide the actor with a legitimate plotline are the good ones.

Wrap-up

Whether your actors are successful or not the first time through their rehearsed exercise is not the issue. Building in your actors a process by which they are willing and able to make effective acting choices is far more important in the long run. In the places where your student actors clearly run into trouble with their exercises, your student audience can eventually make suggestions that will provide clarity or heightened power to the performing actors and their story line. In this way, everyone's acting brain muscles will be flexed, stretched, and strengthened. The exercise can then be repeated, using the contributed input. Undoubtedly, the second time through will be a demonstration of growth in both the story and the actors performing it.

Whisper Down the Lane

Remember that classic gangster movie *White Heat* with James Cagney? It's the one where Cagney blows up with the refinery at the end of the movie while screaming "Top of the world, Ma!" That scene is always shown whenever gangster movie retrospectives play on television. But there is another equally classic segment from that film. It is the one in which Cagney finds out, while serving a sentence in prison, that his mother has died. What makes it a classic is that Cagney gets the news during a meal in the dining hall. Because it is a maximum security prison, none of the inmates are permitted to talk. The message gets to Cagney after it has been whispered mouth to ear countless times down the institutional dining table at which the cons are sitting. The camera pans from face to face like an avalanche picking up momentum as the message moves down the endless bench. When Cagney finally hears the news, so much suspense and expectation have been built up that his response must be gigantic to prevent his big moment from being anticlimactic. Cagney, as he always does, rises to the occasion. First, he takes in the information as his characteristic migraine begins its painful ascent.

When the headache becomes unbearable, Cagney staggers up on the table, hands pressing against his exploding head. He then reels violently along the table's wooden surface blasting tin cups and plates oozing with prison grub in all directions. It is a truly memorable piece of film.

One of the reasons the sequence is so memorable, of course, is that the always reliable Cagney compellingly pulls off his over-the-top acting choices so entertainingly. But another is the way the message itself becomes a character in the scene. We literally watch the message travel from convict to convict as though it were a tangible item. What gives the message its shape, however, is the way each convict specifically takes in, reacts to, and then passes on the information. In other words, what the audience sees is a series of physical actions, each having a beginning, middle, and end, a sequence of powerful ministories that, when put together, tell a much bigger and compelling one.

The party game known as Whisper Down the Lane, or more recently as Telephone, provides essentially the same situation as the scene described above. A group of individuals are seated next to each other in a line. A message is whispered to the first person in the line who then must whisper the message in the ear of the next person, and so on until the message is repeated down the line to the last person. The final person must then repeat the message aloud so that everyone can hear it. The last person's message is then compared with the original message-giver's— usually with hilarious results. But Whisper Down the Lane is a game that, for actors, can provide much more than an entertaining diversion; the game offers a framework to practice and reinforce many of the most important basic skills they will be called upon to employ.

Purpose

Whisper Down the Lane requires its players to listen carefully, to speak clearly, to concentrate, to stay in the moment, and to focus on objectives rather than simply showing off for an audience. But more important, the game can provide both the players and observers with the opportunity to develop their skills in choosing and playing physical actions that are clear and dramatically interesting. It can also help develop their ability to create choices that have dramatic throughlines or, more specifically, develop their ability to play actions that have beginnings, middles, and ends. In addition, the game will eventually drive home to the students engaged in it the importance of the "magic if" and the need to re-create, rather than simply repeat, their work if it is to stay fresh and believable.

Method
ROUND 1
The first round of the game is played as described above. The teacher should provide the first person with a message long and intricate enough that it can become confused as it is passed from player to player. It is better to make up an original message than to use a familiar phrase or proverb. An original message will ensure that the listeners are actually listening to what is being said rather than reconstructing a message based on the parts they have clearly heard. The nonparticipating members of the class should be instructed to carefully observe what they see because a discussion will follow the game. The class should also be reminded that since Whisper Down is being played in an acting class, the game obviously means more than what it does when being played at a party. They should be instructed to look for its acting significance.

DISCUSSION
When the round is over, solicit the class for their observations and responses. It might be effective to write their significant ones on the board. Eventually their list should include the following:

The message itself could practically be seen being passed.

The repeated message had specific and distinct sections.

These sections were clearly observable when watching the game.

The observable sections provided information about the message itself, about the receiver, and about deliverer.

The sections of the process included:

- the delivery of the message
- the receipt of the message
- the reaction to the message
- a clear transition by the player from acting as receiver to deliverer

Since the observing class members cannot hear the message being delivered, it follows then that what they come to know about the message and the characters in the game comes exclusively from what the performers do. The audience follows the sequence of events from the physical actions they observe; they understand the events and their significance because the physical actions are strongly and clearly played, a moment at a time.

ROUND 2

Once the discussion is over, ask the observing students to switch places with those who have just played. When they are in place and ready, tell them and the nonplaying students that you will be giving the first person in line the same message that you gave the first group. Since everyone already knows what the message is, the responses of the players will not be spontaneous reactions this time; rather, they will be acting choices based on what they already have observed and discussed previously.

In all probability the resulting scene will be less believable, less clear, and less interesting. It will also probably contain several moments of bad acting, bad listening, and exaggerated physical action. In other words, it will provide a wonderful springboard for a discussion on what good acting is and how to do it.

In the discussion following this round, the participants and the observers will quickly point out that the listening that went on this time was far less apparent. Since everyone already knew the message, the actors were probably busy thinking about their clever responses rather than listening in the moment. They focused on their reaction instead of taking in the information. This is exactly what too many actors do during scene work and in performance as well. But the savvy audience easily recognizes the difference. Acting that is not reactive in the moment is not believable and often is not understandable either.

When you ask your observers to analyze what went wrong, they will probably recognize that the clarity and believability they saw in the first spontaneous exercise resulted from seeing a throughline of moments consisting of beginnings, middles, and ends that clearly transitioned from one to the other. The actors trying to re-create the effect of the first game simply forgot to include all this in their work.

ROUND 3

Further discussion will lead the students back to the list they compiled after watching the first spontaneous round. They will realize they assumed all the components from the list would simply be in their work without thinking about it. Of course, just the opposite is true. Now they are ready to try again. Ask your players to take a few moments to score out their actions specifically. They might even try writing their physical action score down to make sure they do not forget any part of the throughline they will have to play. When they are confident that they know all the things they have to do, ask them to repeat the exercise, but be sure to remind them that before they do anything, they must be willing to listen to the message and stay in the moment. They must be willing to adjust their actions in accordance with the input they get.

DISCUSSION

Because the actors will be forced to be specific about what they do this time through, the exercise will no doubt be strikingly better than the last time. There will be moments with beginnings, middles, and ends. There will be a logical progression of actions. The moments that are important will be clearly delineated, and overall, the acting will be more interesting and more believable. The power and utility of using physical actions as an acting tool will be dramatically made to your students.

ROUND 4

When the follow-up discussion of Round 3 is completed, your students will be ready to play again. After your actors switch positions, inform them that you will be giving them a message that is very funny. Instruct them to pay close attention and to remember all the things they have learned from the first few rounds. As soon as you say "funny message," their expectations will be aroused, and even before you begin telling the first person in line what the message is, there will be an atmosphere unlike the ones earlier. When you whisper in the first person's ear, instead of a message, tell him that there will be no message. Tell him to react as though a funny message were being delivered, and then pass along the same set of instructions to the next person in line.

If your group is real sharp, the exercise might proceed through several message passes before the game breaks down, but it is more likely that after the first pass, your players will be shocked and surprised by the turn of events. Once this happens, they will break concentration and make clear to the watchers that something is amiss. Obviously, after this happens, the illusion of reality in the game is completely destroyed, and it will have to be stopped.

DISCUSSION

The two important acting concepts that are highlighted are the need for concentration, and, once again, the need to listen in the moment. The disciplined actor will be able to take in the surprise set of instructions while at the same time maintaining the illusion that all is proceeding well in the game. Even though the actor is forced into making instantaneous adjustments, the need to keep the audience believing in the situation is critically important. Onstage, things seldom go completely as planned. Surprises are commonplace in live theater, and the actor must be able to roll with the punches, no matter how surprised he may be.

Round 5

When the discussion following the breakdown is complete, begin again. But this time instruct your players that they must have a subtext for the pretend message being delivered. Since no message will actually be passed this time, they each need to invent the funny message the audience is supposed to be seeing passed. Each of the actors must hear and react to something, the more specific the better. Those players who respond without hearing any message, or any specific one, no matter how big their reaction, will be performing, not reacting in the moment. Chances are they will come off less believable than the players who took the time to make up and listen to a specific imaginary one.

Discussion

As you would with a regular game of Whisper Down the Lane, at the end have the last person stand and recite the message she heard. Most of the time that last person will be shocked that you actually asked to hear the message. Most of the time that last person will be unable to tell you any message because she simply did not hear one. In spite of the instruction at the beginning of the round, the actor simply generalized a response in her mind and performed a reaction. In all probability, that is just how it looked too. Usually this last student will confess to having failed to invent a message, or will try to put into words the fuzzy generalized message idea that she had in mind. Either way, it is clear to the students watching that being specific at every moment onstage is important. The students who were specific with themselves will usually be the ones that seemed the most clear, believable, and interesting to the audience.

ROUND 6

After this discussion, your students are ready to play again. By now they should have specific messages to react to, so their work should be clearer and better acted. But there may still be one major flaw in the work that keeps it from being totally convincing. Ask your observing students if they can pinpoint this flaw. After some tap dancing, they will eventually make the observation that the reactions by the individuals in the line were not consistent. Each actor seemed to receive a different message even though it was supposedly the same one. In fact, this is absolutely true, but if the game is to be believable, then all individual reactions must be consistent with those of the others in the line.

DISCUSSION

Ask your class how the illusion of consistency can be achieved. Eventually, they will conclude that the length of the message must be consistent and the points at which the listener responds (the funniest parts of the message) need to be consistent as well. When the game is played at a party, the length and response points become apparent to the audience as the message is passed along. Therefore, the length of the message is critical in making the audience believe the acting progression. By watching and listening closely, the actors can discover when and where to react and to find a consistency that will make the audience believe in the reality. Of course, you can point out that listening onstage with both ears and eyes is always critical.

ROUND 7

Have your players and observers switch again. This time tell the entire group what the new hilarious message is. Tell them all at the same time. Then begin the game as before without really passing along any message. Because every player knows what the message is supposed to be this time, the consistency and believability of the game will be much easier to maintain. This, of course, emphasizes the importance of being clear about given circumstances when doing acting work. Obviously, the more specific the shared information, the more believable and uniform the work will be.

LATER ROUNDS

Your class is now ready to replay the game with a variety of messages and circumstances. Each round should further develop the skills already discussed. Try a gross-out message or two. Try a sad message, perhaps similar to the one Cagney received in *White Heat*. Try repeating the same message through a couple of rounds with the goal of developing a group physical action score that can literally serve as a script. Work on isolating the reactions that really work, and build a scene by retaining the good moments and adding new ones as they present themselves. Eventually, a whole scene can be built up, rehearsed, and performed.

Once your students have mastered the basic mechanics, you could ask them to play the game, not as themselves, but as characters different than themselves. For this they will need to isolate a personality trait or two that can be converted to physical actions. For instance, if a particular student has chosen to be a shy spinster, her reaction to a gross-out message or a joke in bad taste might be far different than the actor's own personal reaction. In other words, Stanislavski's "magic if" will now come into play. Your students will have to ask themselves "What would I do if I were this character in this situation?" Your students will have to answer that question to find physical choices that not only tell the story of the scene, but reveal who the character is as well. It will be necessary for your students to make choices that they can convert into clear actions the audience can read.

Wrap-up

Finally, Whisper Down the Lane can evolve into a game that your students can play on their feet. By creating a set of given circumstances, a message can be relayed from one character to another until the intended receiver of the message is reached. This variation will allow your students to physicalize the game in a way not possible when sitting in a line. For instance, suppose a message is passed from courtier to courtier in a palace in sixteenth-century England. The message is passed on until it reaches the king on his throne. A variety of physical choices consistent with the given circumstances can be developed by your students that will support the time and place as well as the content of the message. Suppose, for instance, that the message being passed to the English king is that his son, the prince, is dead. The message is of such import, that every messenger along the way would need to take in, react, and adjust to the received message before passing it along to the next messenger. The messenger who must tell the king his son is dead is indeed in a very dramatic situation, requiring skill, courage, and diplomacy.

The situational possibilities are endless. With a little imagination, common sense, and discipline for craft, Whisper Down the Lane can offer up many lessons about the tools an actor must master.

Conflict and Objectives

Whether an actor is working with or without a script, the basic fundamental of storytelling must always be observed, and fundamental number one is the need to identify the conflict where it exists or create conflict when it does not. Drama is action and action is always dependent on the engine called *conflict*.

Types of Conflict

As you probably recall from earlier exercises, there are four basic types of conflict that provide the springboard for storytelling. The first, internal conflict occurs when a character debates with herself about what to think or feel, or must decide a course of action to pursue. The second type of conflict occurs when a character is pitted against nature—snowstorms, fires, natural disasters. The third arises when a character goes against the rules of society. Taking a stand against a political or religious institution or a set of unjust laws would be examples of this kind. In the fourth, a character finds himself in opposition to another character, and this other character provides an obstacle that stands in the way of achieving some goal.

Conflict to Objective

Stanislavski, on whose theories of acting most of our contemporary acting craft is still based, understood the power of conflict. Even in his early work, the great Russian master noted the important connection between what an actor chooses to do and its relation to the script being brought to life onstage.

Stanislavski came to believe that what a character does in a play is far more important than what she feels. Actions are controllable, reliable, and repeatable. Emotions are not. The story related in a play is the result of choices made by the actor based on the overall idea behind the play and the action the playwright sets down to support that idea. Because the playwright has already carefully interwoven the action and its idea, the strength of their interconnection will be in operation at every moment and in every facet of the work.

Stanislavski came to believe that playing actions and doing specific tasks onstage were the cornerstones of acting craft. In fact, most of his later work centered on the storytelling aspects of acting and, specifically, on the use of conflict. His invention of one of the basic tools of acting—*playing objectives*—comes directly from his understanding of dramatic conflict and his own appreciation for its use by good playwrights.

Even though most young actors today are familiar with playing objectives (also known as *intentions* or *needs*), many of them often find it difficult to work with them. Some have no idea how to go about choosing a useful objective; others choose ones that are seemingly ineffective and are quickly forgotten when working. An actor's inability to use objectives often results from failing to use the script as a guide. Too often actors select their objectives without fully understanding what the dramatic situation is in the overall play, in the scene, or even in a particular moment.

A character's need or objective results from the conflict she faces or the obstacles that stand in her way. The actor playing that character must determine what she needs to do to triumph over that opposing force or obstacle. But the actor must first recognize and understand what the conflict is. In other words, if an actor can figure out what the conflict is between her and her acting partner in a scene, she will be able to figure out what she must do to win what is needed. That is the actor's objective. Further, if the actor playing the character keeps in mind that winning what she needs is a full-time job onstage, she will be less likely to forget the objective while playing out a scene. All her choices will be clear, strong, and interesting because they are serving the dramatic situation, not going against it.

The Power Game

I first played this game as a freshman in my MFA in acting program. It is one of the few acting exercises from that period of my training that I remember. Given the fact that my professor at the time, though a good director, was a terrible teacher, I suspect that the game I played then and the one I am about to describe are somewhat different. Over the years I have played the game countless times with my own students and have modified it several times because I now know its potential for teaching. Ironically, at the time I played and watched my first series of contests as a student, I'm not sure I truly understood the game's significance for actors. But the fact is I still have strong memories of the game, and I can still remember several of the contests that the members of my class engaged in. We may not have played it quite the same way that I will describe to you, but we played it to the hilt once we saw how it worked. In all probability, your students will, too. But your students will have the advantage of your being able to explain the game's significance in acting terms. What a picture is to a thousand words, this exercise is to the acting concepts it demonstrates.

Purpose

The Power Game demonstrates with absolute clarity the benefits an actor enjoys when playing an acting objective clearly and specifically onstage. These benefits are obvious to trained, experienced actors, but beginning actors often pay little more than lip service to their stated objective, preferring instead to slip into an emotional state, rely on a spontaneous impulse, or simply react to another actor with no real purpose. Because the stated purpose of The Power Game is to win, players are automatically forced into keeping their objective in mind at all times. The problem, of course, then becomes finding a tactic or series of tactics that will allow them to do that. That is where the real learning comes in. Finding a way to win, moment by moment, beat by beat, scene by scene, throughout the play is the task actors continuously face when doing a role properly. Overcoming obstacles and momentary defeats, adjusting to new information, and changing strategies are all part of the throughline of a character. Situationally, the terrain your student actors face in The Power Game is totally analogous, as they will quickly discover. But without knowing how to win, without knowing what is required to win, your student actors will feel naked on the stage, while an audience watches to see how they deal with their embarrassing, raw exposure.

Method

The game is played by two students at a time. Each pairing can be called a round or a contest. The winner of each round will be determined by a vote of the audience watching. This vote should be taken after the players themselves select whom they thought the winner was. The rules of The Power Game are simple and should be explained exactly in the manner quoted below. The rules may be repeated ad infinitum, but never, I repeat, never explain the rules. They explain themselves. Any amplification of the rules should come as a by-product of the discussion that follows each round of the game. So, here's the script of what you should tell your class by way of instruction: This game is called

The Power Game. The object is to win. The game is over when one of the players speaks or touches the other.

And that's it. Those are the rules. The discussion that follows the voting at the end of the contest should center on the reasons for picking one contestant over the other. The discussion will often prove to be as exciting, interesting, and informative as the game itself. Both the contests and the ensuing discussions will become more sophisticated and specific as the participants and audience learn from each round that is played.

ROUND 1

The first two contestants, usually strong and enthusiastic students if they are volunteers, have a rough time. They are the Lewises and Clarks, blazing an acting trail for the rest of the class. After you repeat your scripted instructions for their benefit and announce the game has begun, they will probably hesitate, laugh nervously at each other, and stare a bit. Finally, one of them will make some arbitrary gesture or movement toward the other. What will happen then is unpredictable. In some cases, one or both of the actors will stumble on some action that the other can pick up on and repeat or amplify. For instance, if one actor feints aggressively toward the other, the other might back off, then feint forward, or he might simply retreat. He might also remain passive or choose to ignore the advance altogether. Sometimes the initial response of the second player will lead to another aggressive action by the first player that causes the same action to continue or escalate. At other times the original action will be arbitrarily dropped, which will lead to another uncomfortable pause in the action and another embarrassed hesitation on the part of the players.

The point that the audience will come to realize—before the contestants themselves do—is that the game is far more interesting and clear when the contestants are playing a particular action with commitment. Further, they will notice that when the actors engage in give and take the transactions are interesting to watch and far more understandable. When the contestants are engaged with each other, despite lack of understanding on their part, the audience comes to see all their actions as interconnected and, therefore, meaningful. Because the actions are seemingly connected, audience members begin to draw conclusions about the actors' relationship with each other. They also begin to draw conclusions about the purpose of the sometimes arbitrary actions they are seeing. Because the game is called The Power Game and because they know that the object of the game is to win, they are looking for a winner even as the players themselves are trying to win. They have consciously or unconsciously determined that the winner will be the one who has exerted the most power. The audience is filling in the gaps in the given circumstances and plot. That's where the fun in the discussion sits.

How long you let the first round go is entirely up to you. If absolutely nothing interesting is going on, you might tell the contestants that only a minute remains. This could provoke them into suddenly making big or interesting choices, but it might not. During that last-minute countdown the game will become more interesting anyway because of the imposed time element. The audience will find the situation dramatically enhanced even if the players contribute nothing to the situation. Imposing a time element increases the stakes and creates conflict. In other words, the stakes have been increased. The audience, if not the actors, begins to realize how important conflict is to an actor and to the story unfolding onstage. Without this dramatic conflict there is little or no story, and that, simply put, is not interesting to watch.

DISCUSSION
The discussion about who won always centers on the concept of power. When asked, the contestants themselves often have opposite views on who won, and often, since they are the ones who participated, they have very strong views at that.

Often in the first round Player A will attempt to assert power by threatening to touch Player B. If B attempts to get away, then A asserted power. If, however, B ignores A or offers no resistance, many in the audience will perceive that B has demonstrated greater power than A and will vote for B. Such a vote often surprises the players. They are shocked to discover that the voting audience has seen things very differently.

What the actors don't necessarily realize, but is quite clear to many in the audience, is that there is also power in the way someone responds to brute force. The passive resistance of the followers of Ghandi or Martin Luther King have demonstrated this time and again. Turning the other cheek to aggression or ignoring it altogether can also demonstrate power. The perception of power often depends on the specific give and take between the parties engaged in the conflict and who is perceived as the good guy and the bad guy.

The players learn that audience perception is far more important than what they themselves may feel. For many actors this realization opens the door to a new awareness about an actor's relationship to an audience. The lesson to emphasize here is that the audience must get the story being told, so the choices being made onstage must produce the desired effect on the audience. Otherwise, a production is likely to miss the mark.

No matter how the audience votes, the beat during which A threatens to touch B is a success because there is conflict. This beat is simple, clear, and exciting. The audience understands the situation, takes sides, and becomes absorbed in finding out what the outcome will be. That is good storytelling, the kind that makes a play compelling and an actor get noticed. Further, once the actors understand their relationship, they start to respond to each new action. Their actions start to have beginnings, middles, and ends. They first take in the new information provided by their adversary, decide on a response, and finally respond. This creates the illusion of reality. It simulates what real persons do from moment to moment in real life. But when a single action is played onstage, rather than the random actions people often execute in life, reality is heightened and made specific in the way good theater must.

LATER ROUNDS

The more rounds are played, the more the students learn about playing objectives simply, clearly, and fully. They come to see how taking in information, weighing it, and responding to it in a way that an audience can understand is critically important. Taking the time to show this to an audience goes a long way toward making an actor's time onstage compelling. It also creates watchable, understandable moments. Once your students realize the importance of having an objective in mind before they start the game, they will provide themselves with an acting game plan that works far more effectively and reliably than winging it. The Power Game will now begin to take off. Your students will bring choices to the exercise that will immediately create conflict. This in turn will lead to clearer relationships onstage and may even contribute to creating given circumstances. Before too many rounds are played, you will probably be witnessing exercises that seem more like scenes than an acting game. This will all result from your students bringing specific choices to the game.

Miscellaneous Information

When touching or speaking occurs, you must immediately end the game. Those are the rules. Touching and speaking usually happen accidently. The players have come too close to each other perhaps, or maybe they have gotten so invested in the game that they touch or speak out of frustration or some other emotion. Speaking means words, by the way, not spontaneous grunts, moans, or screams. The first time touching or speaking occurs and you ask for a discussion and a vote, many in the audience will be surprised. The player who spoke or touched, they will say, lost the game. That's in the rules. When that happens, you will point out that the rules say nothing about losing or winning; the rules say the game is over when someone speaks or touches. This will allow you to get into a discussion on the importance of listening closely—listening for what is said, not for what you think is being said. This is an important concept to be learned by actors. It can prevent jumping to obvious and boring choices when reading a script, for instance. A script should be read for what is there, not for what careless actors may think is there. Being aware that things don't always mean what they seem to on the surface can lead to a demonstration on the importance of making strong, clear moments onstage. A single good acting moment may be far more powerful than simply ice skating through a beat.

After the discussion on speaking and touching, for instance, I sometimes ask a student to play a round with me. As soon as the game starts, I may do something strong and obnoxious to my opponent. With high school seniors, I have given the finger. My opponent and the audience are usually both delighted and shocked. I immediately follow that with speaking or touching my adversary. What a one-two punch! Clearly, the game is over, and unless my class is angry at me, they vote me the winner unanimously. My choice was so powerful and complete that my adversary was left speechless and unable to respond. The whole contest took ten seconds, and my exercise is the one they'll talk about first and remember the longest. The single, strong acting moment onstage is worth far more than several beats of the boring.

A final important concept that The Power Game brings out is that winning and losing onstage is a misnomer. Does losing the game mean a student failed as an actor? Of course not. The point here is that winning and losing is often predetermined by the script. The cowboy/actor who loses the gunfight didn't fail to win his acting objective. He may have gotten killed, but the important thing is he tried to win the gunfight with all his heart. The conflict makes the gunfight exciting, and the success of the acting depends equally on the loser as well as the winner. Ultimately, your students will come to realize this as well. Who is voted the winner in The Power Game is really irrelevant. Whether their round of The Power Game created a good story— one that was exciting to watch and dramatically clear and interesting—is what determines the real winners onstage. The actors who can create such stories are the ones who are hired, the ones who get to do the acting work.

Wrap-up

In conclusion, The Power Game can provide you and your class with many exciting moments on the stage. Be patient until your students get the hang of it. Remember, too, that a discussion on why something is not interesting onstage can be as profitable as one discussing why everything is so wonderful. In time, your students will come up with some thrilling conflicts to play out before your eyes. I have, in my time, seen blackboard poetry contests, piano playoffs, tap dancing frenzies, and even an "I dare you to take something else off" challenge. Let me know what amazing things you end up witnessing.

Stealing Scenes

Whether actors have mastered their craft through an inside-out process (emotional truth) or an outside-in process (physical action) or a combination of each, the fact remains that there comes a time early on in the process when the actor must ask himself "what am I doing here, why am I doing this, what is my intention, what is my need, what is my action, what do I want?!" Any approach to acting eventually requires the actor to figure out what his objectives are and how to play them, no matter what he calls them. Otherwise, the actor's journey through a play ends up being aimless and unclear. I often tell my own students that acting is not the same as reality; it just looks like it is—if it's done well. This is especially true during rehearsals, when the actor is exploring and going through a process of selection trying to discover what works. After all, it's harder to stay fully in the moment when an observant critical inner voice is constantly commenting about the choices you are making. I also tell my students that what feels really good for the actor is not always what works best for the audience. If the audience does not get what the actor is doing onstage, then no matter how good it feels for the actor, there is something wrong with it. The actor's primary purpose is, after all, to serve the play by communicating it well to the audience.

As the previous exercise demonstrated, when an actor plays an objective onstage, she must simplify what, in life, would remain much more complicated. In life, for instance, when we get involved in a heated argument we usually fight to win. In acting terms, winning the argument becomes our objective. But in real life we do not usually think about this. It happens intuitively because it is fueled by emotion not intellect. Our arguments are often sloppy, illogical, and circuitous. It usually takes a lot longer to get to the point. But a well-written play has structure and organization, and the playwright has worked hard to keep only the essentials in the dialogue. A well-trained actor realizes this when he studies his script. He probably figures out the throughline of an "argument scene" by first discovering the conflict that fuels it and eventually getting a grip on an objective that keeps him connected with the other actor or actors in the scene with him. The actor decides that his objective in the scene is to win the argument, but unlike people in real life, he keeps that objective actively in mind as he goes through the moments of the scene: first, during his private preparation, and then later, when he rehearses with his partner. His choices will always reflect and support his objective because, unlike in life, his purpose is to keep only the essentials—to maximize the clarity and power of the story being told dramatically.

The seeming paradox is that while we ask our acting students to play their objectives at all times, we also ask them to stay in the moment, to listen to their partners, and to trust themselves. We tell them that if they stay in the moment and listen, their work will be spontaneous and fresh and it will never be exactly the same twice, and that this skill is what makes the best actors so fascinating. The problem, of course, is that when our actors focus on the listening and react with genuine spontaneity, they sometimes forget the objectives they set out to play. When that happens, the clarity, shape, and dramatic power built into a scene is often diminished or lost completely. Actors must be able to do both at the same time; this discipline can and must be mastered. Actors must learn to act onstage with a spontaneity that comes from listening in the moment, but they must also react with choices that keep them moving toward their objective.

Purpose

The exercise that I call Stealing Scenes provides student actors with the opportunity to work on these seemingly paradoxical acting skills. It requires them, just as a script does, to play their objectives fully while at the same time requiring them to stay in the moment and react to every new piece of information. Stealing Scenes further requires them to subdivide their objectives into smaller tactics to overcome the obstacles that interfere with their achievement. The game also requires them to:

- pay attention to all established given circumstances

- make choices that are logical and believable

- complete actions that are justified with beginnings, middles, and ends

- develop their ability to use Stanislavski's "magic if" (what would I do if I were this character in this situation?)

Further, Stealing Scenes provides them with the opportunity to come to understand that good acting does not necessarily require the actor to achieve his objective, it merely demands that the actor do everything in his power to achieve it.

Method

Stealing Scenes is a simple situational acting game. It requires three students to play while the rest of the class watches. Two of the three actors are assigned to play robbers trying to steal a treasure from the third actor who lives in a room, apartment, or house represented by the playing area available in your class.

The specific given circumstances—the who, what, where, and when—can be determined by the class, the teacher, the actors, or a combination of the three. When preliminary decisions about the given circumstances have been made, the game begins. Obviously, the objectives of each of the characters is built in. The two robbers want to get the treasure, and the character who lives in the house tries to prevent them from doing it.

Now here's the rub. The teacher or any member of the class may stop the action any time she feels the reality of the situation is being violated. If someone stops the game, however, she must be able to articulate her justification for stopping the action specifically and clearly. A discussion of the point being made should then ensue. Violations of reality include but are not limited to:

- illogical choices by the characters
- disregarding any of the established given circumstances
- adding information to the story that is extraneous or tangential
- behaving in a manner not set up by some earlier action
- ignoring Stanislavski's "magic if"

After the perceived violation has been discussed, the actors must go back to the point in the story where the acting violation occurred (if there is agreement that one has), or the actors must return to the point where the action was halted (if it is decided that no actual violation has been committed). The improvisation continues until the next perceived violation is reported, discussed, and settled. This process continues until the actors get stuck, the story is somehow resolved, or the teacher is forced to end the game. Reasons for ending the game include continuous violations of logic, inability of the actors to concentrate, physical choices that are dangerous to fellow actors, continued inability of the actors to play out the scene without commenting on it (showing the audience that they are really just actors playing characters), and the worst violation of all—choices that are boring to watch.

DISCUSSION

As any experienced acting teacher knows, the things that people do in real life automatically without thinking are often things that are totally forgotten when a person suddenly becomes an actor onstage engaged in a situation. Stealing Scenes provides an object lesson on this point. Certain basic assumptions, things that real robbers and real victims of crime would never forget, for example, are quickly forgotten when your students go from intelligent people to performing actors. A pair of robbers would never hang out outside the victim's house in broad daylight discussing their plans for robbery. A person in this day and age would never simply open her door and let strangers in without a very strong justification. Your student actors, in all probability, will. In fact they will forget all kinds of obvious stuff that the smart people in the audience will immediately pick up on. This is what makes the game so much fun to do and to watch. By playing the game, your students will also get a better sense of what a beat is and how it works. A beat is the length of script during which an actor plays a particular objective or tactic. A beat is over when the objective has been completed successfully, has been abandoned in defeat, or has been replaced by a new objective. The end of a beat must be followed by a transitional moment when the actor takes in that victory, defeat, or new information. At this critical juncture, the actor as character must share with the audience what he is now thinking or feeling; otherwise, his next set of actions will probably be unclear or seem unmotivated to the audience. Often, during these transitional points, a member of the watching class will stop the action because your actors are most likely committing one or more of the violations mentioned above. Those watching often see from the outside what the actors are blind to from within the context of the scene.

Suppose, for example, that the given circumstances set up by you and your class include these:

The intended victim of the crime is a little old lady living in a bad neighborhood who actually has a lot of money hidden in her house.

The robbers are neighborhood kids who are inexperienced but have heard the rumor that she has a treasure stashed somewhere inside.

It is daytime.

You might want to let the little old lady set up her own room since she is going to be the one living there. If she establishes the location of her windows and door, she will have to live with her choices. The same is true of any furniture and props she might select. This will eventually lead to a discussion of her placement choices, both for her use as an actor and the effect these choices have on the audience's ability to see and understand the action. I usually have the little old lady begin first before bringing on the robbers. When your actor is ready, the exercise begins. As the curtain rises, what is she doing? If your actors are like many of my own, she will be doing nothing. You could stop the action and ask her about her choice or lack thereof.

"What are you doing?," you might ask.
"Waiting," she answers.
"Waiting for what?"
"For the robbers to come."
Laughter from the class.

This actually happens quite often. Your actors immediately forget what is obvious to those watching. Your actor is not yet staying in the moment. Her objective of protecting her treasure is not necessarily a playable objective until the situation develops to the point that it becomes one. If protecting her treasure is not yet a playable action, what should she be doing? Your actor must come up with an action or objective because it is the actor's responsibility to be active or interesting to watch at every moment. The action selected should somehow contribute to the story either by moving the plot forward or by contributing some useful character information. By useful I mean information that will help make clear the reasons for a later choice or help explain her unfolding personality. Often students choose to have the old lady watch and react to a television soap opera. This provides the actor with an interesting action to play. Watching a TV soap allows her to respond vocally to what she is seeing, which in turn tells us even more about her character. It also makes clear that the action is taking place in the daytime.

On the other hand, your old lady could choose to be obsessed with her treasure. She might want to protect it by staying close, or rechecking its security periodically. If the treasure is money, she might want to count it or rehide it or cover it more securely. This obsession might lead her to take chances to protect her valued possession.

Now, what about the robbers? If, as set up in the given circumstances above, they are callow young thieves from the neighborhood, the way they seek the treasure should reflect their lack of experience. Will they immediately try to break into the house in spite of the fact that the little old lady is there? Will they not realize that the little old lady is home? Would they attempt to break in before checking? What does this say about their intelligence level if they do? If they are kids from the neighborhood, do they know the old lady? Does she know them? Would they try to get her to let them in before attempting to break in? How badly do they want or need the treasure? What are they willing to do to get it? Is this a prank or serious business? Are they capable of violence? Are they willing to use violence? Is the treasure worth using violence? If they decide to break in, do they know how? Could they do it without being heard? Without being caught? Once inside, do they have a strategy for finding the treasure? These and hundreds of other questions can and will come into play as the characters and situations develop. Every new action should grow out of the previous moment without violating the logic of the situation in any way. As the process proceeds in its halting fashion, beats will be created, established through repetition, and occasionally altered to accommodate new plot and character information. Use your own judgment about when the particular exercise is running out of steam. At that point, you could select a new set of actors to continue the established scene, or you could start from the beginning using the same given circumstances (if they're good ones and haven't yet been exhausted), or you could create a whole new set of circumstances. Here is a partial list of variations that have worked for me:

The robbery victim could be legally blind. (She could actually be blindfolded.)

The treasure could actually be placed somewhere on the set so that the robbers can actually find or fail to find it.

The robbery victim could have a gun on hand.

The robbers could have a gun or knife. (At what point does the threat of physical violence become necessary in the scene, if ever?)

The robbery could be attempted in a very well-to-do neighborhood.

The victim of the robbery attempt could be a child. (Try it at various ages.)

The robbers could be real professionals. (To be believed, the robbers' choices will have to reflect that fact—no easy task.)

Vary the time of day, month, and year. (A night robbery is different than a day robbery. Lingering outside a house in the throes of winter is far different than during a balmy spring day. A more genteel time could make a victim less expectant of being robbed, the robbers more polite and less prone to violence.)

These and several hundred other possible variations will completely change the dynamics of the robbery situation, which will, in turn, force your students to redefine what is logical, believable, and pertinent to the story. If your robbers are armed, chances are they will want to use their weapon immediately. Your young actors will find using a weapon to be an exciting prospect. But will they be justified in using the gun simply because they have it? If they are young toughs, perhaps. But if the victim is old and blind, won't she be relatively easy to over-power if the robbers manage to get inside her house? What tactics would robbers use if they discover their victim is a child? At what age is a child savvy enough to handle the problem she is confronted with. At what point does the victim call the police? How will the robbers handle the issue of the phone? If the police have been called, what should the robbers do? How believably do the robbers handle the issue of finding the money? How much money makes it worth the risk of being caught? What are the given circumstances that justify the risk? How can the actors make the audience believe that their risk-taking choices are indeed justified?

Wrap-up

You and your students will find countless reasons to stop the action for interesting and profitable discussion. They will become far more aware of the cause-and-effect relationship between given circumstances and action on the stage. In no time, you will notice they are beginning to think like actors. In fact, you will probably discover that many of them start to apply this same kind of thinking to their scripted work. But even if some of them don't immediately, your students will surely find the process toward a completed Stealing Scene, like an adventure through a maze or puzzle, a compelling journey to undertake. They will also discover that the objective attempted but never completed can still provide the engine for exciting work onstage.

Musical Chairs

In the previous chapters, I have described a number of acting exercises that have employed basic acting concepts. The exercises described have included using physical actions, playing objectives strongly and clearly, telling the best possible dramatic story by using conflict and Stanislavski's "magic if." I have also referred to other acting concepts, such as playing beginnings, middles, and ends; acting the transitional moment (victories, defeats, and discoveries); making choices based on usable given circumstances; taking risks and playing for high stakes; and defining and playing relationships with specificity.

The game of Musical Chairs, the same game you played at birthday parties and dances when you were growing up, can, when properly implemented, become an excellent acting exercise employing all the above concepts and acting tools. With proper side coaching from you, and a little imagination all around, Musical Chairs offers unlimited acting possibilities.

Method

The setup for the acting exercise version of Musical Chairs is just like the setup in the original party game. Chairs are placed side by side in a line, with each adjacent seat facing in the opposite direction of the previous chair. The line of chairs should number one less than the number of people actually playing the game. A cassette player, radio, or some other source of music must be used for the game. When the music is turned on, all contestants circle around the line of chairs until the music stops. At that time the players must scramble to sit in a chair. The player without a seat is eliminated from the game. Each time a contestant is eliminated, one chair should also be removed so that there is always one less chair than the number of players. The game proceeds until there is only one chair and two contestants remaining. The winner is determined by who sits in the remaining chair.

GAME VARIATIONS

Here is a partial list of rules that you could use to supplement the basic format of the game. Feel free to add your own twists, or combine rules as you see fit.

A player is eliminated if he stops moving in a forward direction for any reason.

A player is eliminated if he touches a chair before the music stops.

A player is eliminated if he touches another contestant before the music stops.

A player is eliminated if she passes another player while circling.

A player may move around the chairs as quickly or slowly as she likes.

A player may cut between chairs to gain an advantage.

A player must move at a particular tempo or in a particular mode (jumping, hopping, skipping, on toes, knees).

ROUND 1

You will be surprised by the commitment and energy your students immediately demonstrate with the game. They will probably bring to the exercise a memory of past musical chair games and, unlike the response with some other acting exercises, the memory of the game's potential will keep them from the usual tepid initial reception. In addition, by manipulating the rules and adding to the given circumstances of the game, you can turn a simple but exciting contest into an acting event that will provide your students with a wealth of acting problems to deal with. Remind your students that they are not playing Musical Chairs simply for fun. It is important that they keep in mind that the game is an acting exercise and that they should constantly try to relate what happens in the game to the acting process. For instance, they can be reminded that trying to win the game is like trying to accomplish an objective in an acting situation. Trying various strategies to win is essential, such as keeping close to an available chair. A decision to play the game in this manner is like the tactics an actor uses to achieve an acting objective. Another strategy might be to keep an eye on the music provider for clues as to when the music will stop. This is not unlike focusing on an acting partner who provides the immediate source of conflict in a scene. The analogies are infinite. Keep your students thinking.

ROUND 2: UPPING THE STAKES

Up the stakes by offering a prize to the last remaining contestant. If winning can mean more to the players than the simple victory itself, your students may change the way they invest in the game. Your contestants must now make decisions about what the prize means to them. How invested in winning will they be for a quarter? A dollar? $25? $100?

Different degrees of investment in winning will provide varying degrees of commitment to the game, so provide your students with prizes that will cause them to make different acting decisions. Remind them that making decisions about the prize is not enough. They must also make their attitudes about the prize clear so an audience would understand what they are doing during the game. They must choose physical actions that will communicate their level of commitment toward and their attitude about winning.

For instance, if the prize is a pair of tickets to a Back Street Boys concert, and Player A hates the Back Street Boys, how might he play the game? Would his acting objective be to lose the game intentionally? Suppose he is clever with a dollar? Would he try like hell to win the tickets so he could sell them later? Suppose Player B has a boyfriend who likes the Back Street Boys even though she does not? Would she try to win the tickets to please him, or would she choose instead to selfishly avoid the concert by losing. Character can be demonstrated most clearly by the actions an actor chooses to play. Get your actors to think their choices through. This is an important element in an actor's preparation.

ROUND 3: USING THE MUSIC

Musical chairs can also be an excellent way to do movement training with your actors. By varying the kind of music you use during each round, you can produce an awareness in your actors of their bodies that they might not ordinarily have and get them to use their bodies in innovative ways. For instance, as themselves in the game, they might not respond to the rhythm of a rock beat or to the driving beat of a techno-pop selection. They might not be susceptible to the fluid glide of a Strauss waltz or a Tchaikovsky suite. But if you ask them to be characters responding to this musical variety, your actors will produce a much broader range of movement than you thought they possessed. I have seen the most buttoned-down, egghead student suddenly cut loose to a dance number by "the artist formerly known as Prince" once he had the freedom to dance as a character rather than himself. I have seen wallflowers suddenly move with grace and poetry to Debussy when they pretended to be dancers rather than themselves. Ask your students to invent characters for themselves to play during the game, but remind them that along with the "who" they choose to be is the responsibility of making physical choices that demonstrate to an audience what these choices are.

ROUND 4: CHARACTERIZATION

You might ask your students to share with you some descriptive words that best define the character they have chosen to play. They might say, for instance, that they are playing a character who is shy, or belligerent, or hard of hearing, or sexy. These adjectives are all well and good, but how can they translate these descriptive words into actions? And where in the course of the game do they have the opportunity of performing these actions? This is always the challenge to the actor, and within the context of Musical Chairs, it is even more so because of the limited dramatic structure provided by the game.

Take the time to explore with your students available options for translating their character descriptions into actable choices. A shy character might move in a particular way, might have a body language and posture that suggests shyness. The diffident character might avoid eye contact and might react to the music far differently than an aggressive character. The belligerent character might, as part of her objective, try to scare or alienate all those around her, attempting at all times to create conflict. The hard-of-hearing character might move physically toward the source of music whenever possible. There should be no specific right or wrong with regard to your students' choices. The discussion should instead work toward clarity and specificity. If a student has chosen a character that seems impossible to convey even after discussion, she should abandon that choice. The process that got her to reach this conclusion is extremely valuable, however. Acting is a process that involves trial and error. The ability to jettison something that doesn't work is vitally important for an artist.

As your actors play the game as their characters, they will soon discover that the biggest acting moments occur when the music stops or is about to stop. The manner in which the actors handle these moments are the most revealing for the audience. How does the shy character react to the victory of getting the coveted chair or to the defeat of not getting it? What is she willing to do, shyness not withstanding, to get that seat on the chair? The actor may do some surprising things. Are they consistent with the character as a whole? Can the choices be justified? Will the audience believe it?

Your actors must continually evaluate their performance and determine whether they have made the best choices for their character. They must also think about whether their responses are those of the characters playing Musical Chairs or those of the actors themselves, caught up in the moment when the music stops. Again, it is not a matter of being right or wrong, but rather of making the best possible choices. When the sexy female character loses a chair to an attractive male and winds up sitting in his lap, which is more important for her—winning the game or the physical contact? Which choice makes the clearest story? The most interesting story? What can she do physically to complete the moment and make it clear to the audience? The moment the music stops in Musical Chairs can and should become a defining moment for each of the characters playing the game. Actors must become sensitive to this fact. These defining moments help make the individual performance.

LATER ROUNDS: ADDING GIVEN CIRCUMSTANCES

After your students have explored the acting possibilities suggested above, you may want to add more complex given circumstances and develop fuller improvisations, still using Musical Chairs as the premise. For these fuller improvisations, you will need to do more active coaching, stopping the improvisation regularly to explore and review the work going on—developing what works and eliminating what is extraneous or what simply does not work.

The music selections you offer can influence the kind of given circumstances your actors work from. Country or folk music might suggest a Western hoe-down. The cowboys have returned from the cattle drive or another day of community barn building. What relationships do the characters have toward each other, and how can this information contribute to the story in the context of the game? Are two young cowboys vying for the same girl? Is there flirting going on as the game is being played? What do the fathers and mothers think of the display going on before them? What social customs of the time must influence the actors' choices?

Suppose the game takes place in a medieval setting. Gregorian chant, Hildegard von Bingen, or even the alternative group Dead Can Dance can provide the feel of the Middle Ages. Under what circumstances might this game be played in the year 1025? What jumps to mind when one thinks of castles and knighthood?

In one scenario, perhaps the winner of the game is sacrificed to a dragon standing on the far side of the castle walls. As each round is played, another subject knows himself to be saved from the dragon's hungry jaws while those who continue in the game must play against their growing fear of a horrible death.

Or, in another scenario, perhaps a strange but intriguing tradition exists in the kingdom. The prince must choose his bride from the subjects playing the game at a ball. Perhaps it is the winner herself who gets to marry the prince. How do all the individuals participating in the game or watching it fit into the picture? How does each individual react to the new events that occur during the game? What is the nature of the relationships the characters have with each other?

Plot and character are important but so is setting. The setting will require a sensibility about style and influence physical choices. Courtly manners would prohibit certain flamboyant physical choices that might be made in a contemporary setting. Would a damsel allow herself to make physical contact with a young knight? Would the restraint of manners prohibit overt demonstrations of a desire to win? Would good manners prohibit a knight or squire to take the seat that might have been occupied by a slower and more helpless damsel? How do subjects behave in the presence of royalty? How do commoners behave in noble company?

These are the kinds of questions that can and should arise. They will provide you, as your students' coach and teacher, the opportunity to explore how a knowledge of history and social custom is critical to an actor. This segment of the exercise can help to drive this important point home. The world of the play being produced requires an actor to adjust his range of choices in accordance with the customs of the time. What might work in a contemporary setting may fall flat when transferred to another time and another place.

As you watch your group working on the scenarios they invent, you will come up with other times and places into which the format of the game can be placed. Each new set of given circumstances will provide new problems to solve and new situations to play. Only imagination limits the possibilities. But all individual action must be consistent with the basic given circumstances and to the requirements of playing the Musical Chairs game.

Wrap-up

Imagination and story-building can keep this exercise fresh and exciting for quite some time. A simple change in locale can alter tactics, reactions, and physical choices even if other given circumstances remain the same. This sequence of exercises is a wonderful way to keep your young actors engaged and excited; while at the same time giving them the opportunity to think on their feet. Let the music begin!

Murder!

The previous exercises in this chapter have all dealt with that basic engine of drama—conflict. Each should have demonstrated that a good story arises when character objectives are played out in opposition on the stage. The Power Game pointed out clearly that when objectives become strong and specific, actors transform into interesting characters by the tactics they use and the actions they take, as perceived by an audience. Musical Chairs and Stealing Scenes add to this basic premise by requiring actors to define and refine given circumstances and by requiring a specific commitment to tactics, logical progression, and the use of physical action to make clear the storytelling process.

Murder! (also known as Mafia and Wink) uses all the tools we have been working with throughout this chapter and adds the ultimate twist—the one that guarantees maximum dramatic potential. Neither the actors playing out a scenario involving murder, nor the audience watching it, can fail to be drawn into this kind of situation, because life and death is at its very core.

The value of making every acting situation close to life and death has been one of the basic acting tenets of this book. At this point, no one would argue with the premise that it is the actor's responsibility to make the stakes in every dramatic situation as high as possible. But Murder! offers the ultimate stakes as a built-in ingredient. What happens when an actor must respond as though his life is in jeopardy?

From its beginning, the movie business has relied on the fact that life-and-death situations capture both an audience and their pocketbooks. From *Jaws* to *Titanic*, from *Alien* to *Scream*, from *Silence of the Lambs* to *Speed* to *Gladiator*, the question of who will survive has been a bankable magnet to lure huge audiences. So common is this dramatic situation in film and television that the difficulties inherent in acting in it is often underestimated or disregarded altogether by both audiences and, more to the point, beginning actors. The following homicidal exercise can go a long way to reverse that trend.

Purpose

Murder! can and will reinforce the importance of the tools previously presented in this section. These tools include the use of conflict, objectives, tactics, given circumstances, logical progression, the "magic if," and the use of physical actions, etc. The game of Murder! will also develop a better understanding of the power and effectiveness of using high stakes in any acting situation. The game will also expose students to the necessity and difficulty in keeping those stakes seemingly real while playing the given circumstances.

Method

ROUND 1

The object of the game is for the selected murderer to kill as many players as possible before getting caught in the act. For the other players, the object is to survive for as long as possible by actively avoiding being killed. A murder is accomplished when the murderer winks at another player after eye contact between them is firmly made. After a five count, the player winked at must die by dropping to the floor. The game continues until all players have been killed, or until a player who has not been winked at attempts to identify the murderer. When a player thinks she knows who the guilty party is, that player may stop the game to make an accusation. If the accuser is correct, the game is over. If the accuser is incorrect, the game continues, but only after the accuser commits suicide in a humiliating manner while everyone watches.

Begin the game by asking your students to sit in a wide circle. Ask them to close their eyes. While their eyes are closed, remind them that even though they may be familiar with this game, it is now being played in an acting class. Ask them to regard the exercise in acting terms rather than as a party game. Suggest that this means they must focus on what they are doing or choose to do in a manner that is different than the way they have played previously. Ask them to use their acting compasses— that definition of good acting—and apply it to the situation at hand. Once you have made the point that the activity is no longer a simple party game, inform your students that you will walk around the circle several times, and that during your journey you will touch one of them on the top of the head. The person who is touched will be the murderer once the game begins. Be sure to continue circling for some time after you touch someone so that no one can guess the identity of the murderer. When enough time has elapsed after the murderer has been selected, ask your students to open their eyes and stand. When you give them the signal to begin, they are to wander around the playing area (defined by you) in a random manner. The murderer should try to develop an effective strategy for killing without getting caught. The game proceeds as described above.

DISCUSSION
In the first round, your students will focus on eye contact, either making it or avoiding it, depending on whether they are mur-

derers or potential victims and on whether they like risk taking or like to avoid it. In all likelihood, their mood will be spirited to giddy. The game will strike them as silly or fun, and some of your actors will be self-consciously thinking about what they will do if they are winked at. The manner in which they circle will probably in no way reflect the given circumstances of the game— that one of them is about to be murdered. So far so good. They haven't yet learned that a murder is about to take place (because as characters in an acting situation they have not yet learned what the script contains), so their giddy self-consciousness is not completely out of line. However, all that must change, once the first person is killed and drops to the floor.

But it probably won't—at least not for most of your students. Usually, the first person to die will either be laughing or overacting, his dying moment executed with a total disregard for the reality of the situation. Worse, everyone else will start laughing. Many of your students will make lightly critical or humorous comments about the supposedly dramatic action that has just taken place. This reaction will most likely be repeated when the first wrongful accuser has to die in front of the rest of the class. At this point you could either start taking notes on the violations of reality that you are witnessing, or you might ironically comment on what you are seeing. You could also halt the game to make comments, and then allow it to pick up from where you interrupted the action. If you choose the first approach, you will have a lot to talk about when the round is over. If you choose the second approach, some students might be able to adjust their playing in accordance with the point you are making, but most will self-consciously continue to comment on their work and on the fictional situation they are failing to respond to. If you choose the third approach, you can discuss violations of reality on an ongoing basis, by stopping the game as necessary. Concentration, playing the given circumstances as they develop, and a recognition of the major dramatic events become the focal points for discussion in this first round.

Here's a likely progression of the game if you choose the

stop-and-go approach. Because students know the game before they begin, some will start laughing the moment they start walking. These players will need to be reminded to focus on the situation as though it were a real one. They will have to respect the given circumstances necessary for taking the game seriously or create a set of circumstances so that they don't walk around simply waiting to be bumped off. Even if some of your students can't get past the fact that this is an acting exercise, they must still make one of two choices if they are going to create a reality for themselves: either they don't know someone is about to be killed or they do know someone will be murdered and so must avoid eye contact with the other players to avoid being winked at.

Once they are all onboard with a set of circumstances that allows them to concentrate and play their objectives, the game continues until the first murder. At that point it is likely that the victim will laugh as she falls to her death, and it is also likely that others will join that bandwagon. You students will need to be reminded that murder has been committed and that this is a big news item, and a very serious one at that. How would someone react to a murder in such close proximity? Your students will need to begin to make appropriate choices. The actor who is actually killed, on the other hand, must be made to realize that her murder is a wonderful acting opportunity. How should she, could she, die in an interesting and effective manner?

Those who witness the death must respond in a manner appropriate to the kind of death. Is the death process gentle, painful, long, short? Is a wink like being shot, poisoned, or strangled? Does the manner of death suggest natural causes or murder? How do the remaining players react to the body? What do witnesses do with the body? Pick it up? Step over it? Your students may ask you for advice. Try raising given circumstance questions rather than giving a solution. You want to encourage your actors to develop their ability to make choices that are believable and interesting. In this first round, you need not spell out given circumstances for your students to play, but you should encourage them to make believable choices given the far-out circumstances confronting them.

In reality, people who find a body would probably speak to each other, attempt to call the police, or bond in some common action, but in this first round, no group improvisation should be encouraged; talking between students should not be permitted. It will only spark bad acting with hammy dialogue. However, a body is on the floor. Should students simply step over it with obliviousness bordering on the psychotic, or should they react to the horror? Which is the better choice? Which is more believable? Which is more interesting—both to play and to watch?

As each additional person is murdered, the stakes get higher, the given circumstances become more acute. When the first death occurs, a reasonable person might conclude bad luck, accident, or even "vendetta not involving me" was the cause. But as the body count increases, all actors must confront the fact that they are in as much danger as those who died before them. It is the responsibility of each actor to physically demonstrate this logical throughline of thought and feeling. How can each of your students make choices that reflect the increasingly dangerous reality confronting them?

In addition, each time someone dies, it is a major news event, a discovery that each surviving actor must see, come to grips with, and react to. As the realization of personal danger increases, what tactics will each player use to survive? Those students who simply continue to randomly walk through the space are not playing the given circumstances in a believable or compelling manner. What would a person do in similar circumstances? Remind your actors that feelings alone will not read to an audience; nor will they move the story forward. Stanislavski's "magic if" can and should be applied at this point, so that each of your actors can find something to do while continuing to move through the playing area.

The first time the game is played, the murderer will probably not get past five or six murders before the culprit is identified and the game is over. At that point, you can lead a discussion summarizing and reviewing the acting points that were brought out by the game. It is probably a good idea to play the game this way two or three times before complicating the situation. During each repetition of this basic format, you will no doubt see improved acting moments, better concentration, a clearer development of the unfolding story, better deaths, higher stakes, and a bigger variety of reactions to the victims as they drop to their death. In short, your actors will be starting to make the transition from playing a game to acting a story.

ROUND 2

This round can be played in the same manner as the first round. However, unknown to the players, this time when you select the murderer, pick two or even three rather than a solo killer. Do not announce this fact; do not in any way indicate that the game will be slightly different. Just allow the game to unfold. There should be several significant differences this time through.

DISCUSSION

A multikiller game will be far more exciting to play and to watch. The element of surprise and spontaneity will make all the difference. Much of what happens will have an air of uncertainty and desperation, qualities not unlike the response to an actual murderous situation. This round will be more dramatically effective and real—two strong pluses in theatrical work.

The selected killers will quickly become unsure about their role in the game. When players who they have not killed begin to drop, your murderers will go from confident, to confused, and then to desperate. At first, they may be concerned that they are wrecking the game and wonder if they should stop killing. But as they think the situation through, they will usually decide to continue, in spite of the fact that there must be another murderer. Usually, they will pick up the pace of killing while trying to either kill rival murderers or discover who they might be. The murderers will also be unsure whether or not they can be killed by another murderer. This will add to their desperate confusion and likely ensure that their killing pace stays rabid. They may also try to ask you if there can be more than one killer, and if so whether one murderer can kill another. Remain sphinx-like and let them discover their own answer through their actions. Some interesting variations will occur.

Meanwhile, the other players will have little opportunity to think about what they should be doing. The frantic pace of the game this round will have them dropping to the floor so rapidly that much of the self-consciousness that marked their behavior in the first round will disappear. This time, because of the spontaneity, they will simply die when killed, relying on impulses unfiltered by a judging brain. Overall, their deaths will be much more effective. The same will be true for their responses to the death of others. The intense pace of killing will be surprising to them, which will cause reactions that are far more believable and interesting than in the first round and will parallel likely responses to a real situation.

As the round progresses, several players may realize that there is more than one killer, which will force them into finding a more active strategy to stay alive. These strategies include a stronger attempt to locate the killers and a general avoidance of their fellow players. The ensemble's group reaction will create a nightmarish atmosphere that can be extremely interesting for an audience to watch. You will also notice that both silence and active nonverbal responses are far more apparent this round, adding to the atmosphere of fear. You will want to talk about all this with your students.

Your actors will be very excited after playing this first round of multiple killer and will happily discuss what they went through during the course of the game. Once you have isolated all the significant acting elements that made the round work so effectively, try another game with multiple killers, instructing your class to try and use all the things that worked so well previously. Of course, it will be much harder this time to create or, more to the point, re-create all the elements that worked the last time through. But that is, after all, the job of the good actor. An actor in performance is rehearsed and knows what will happen next, but it is her job to stay in the moment and act and react with a combination of knowingness and spontaneity that makes the work exciting, yet clear and effective. When the round is over, you will want to make and reinforce this very important acting concept. Repeat the Round 2 scenario until it grows repetitious.

ROUND 3
This round is an improvisation that allows dialogue and direct interaction between all players. The scenario is just like the basic plot for the movie *House on Haunted Hill*. You can play ghoulish party host, Vincent Price (my reference is to the original movie, not the recent remake). Before the game begins, ask your class to select roles for themselves to play at the party they are about to improvise. They may choose to be party-goers, musicians, cocktail waiters with hors d'oeuvres, or bartenders. The more specific they are, the better. Make sure that there are an ample number of party guests among the participants, and ask your actors to define their characters as much as possible on short notice. Also make sure that job distribution is reasonable so party activities are well balanced. Once your actors have decided on their roles, a murderer should be selected by you in the manner described for previous rounds.

When the selection is over, have your cast begin an improvisation in which they are all strangers attending a party in a large room. They are awaiting the arrival of their host. Allow them to chat and do things that they would do at a real function. When the time seems right, make your entrance as the host. Tell your guests that you have invited them all to spend the night in your mansion, reputed to be haunted. At the stroke of midnight all doors and other venues for escape will be locked. Those who survive the night will be paid $1 million at sunrise. Until that time, they are all to enjoy themselves. The host then leaves.

The game is played in the same manner as before; however, now that dialogue and role-playing are elements, the reality of the situation can and must be better maintained. Feel free to interrupt when violations of logic occur, or when dramatic possibilities are ignored or improperly responded to. The game and improvisation continues until all are dead, or the killer is discovered.

DISCUSSION

The given circumstances and permitted dialogue of the improvisation in this round vastly increase the number of choices available to your actors and will make for a far more complex and interesting story. But these factors will also increase errors in logic, dramatic effectiveness, and believability. Further, because dialogue will now be permitted and heavily employed, what your actors choose as their objectives and how they pursue them will become, not only more important, but obvious to an audience when they fail to meet that objective effectively. As with previous acting exercises, this round should focus on choices that best tell the unfolding story—choices that make that story clear, believable, and exciting for an audience to watch.

In earlier rounds, for instance, after the first player falls to the floor dead, each actor will independently come to the conclusion that a murderer is loose. That may happen immediately or after a few additional murders occur. Once the conclusion is made, that actor's objective becomes simply to stay alive by avoiding eye contact or by trying to become invisible. In this more sophisticated variation, that kind of response simply won't do. Once the first murder occurs, dialogue automatically makes the response a group one, and all subsequent plot progression continues to require a group dynamic. Your players will argue over strategy, develop alliances, make discoveries, draw conclusions, and try and fail as an allied group, or as groups in competition for control.

All acting choices in this round will have to take into account the reactions of all the other players. There can be no acting in a vacuum. In this situation, anything said or done affects the others in the locked chamber. In addition, in this round, there can be no oblivious stepping over bodies. Those that die have been living, breathing acquaintances or friends, and as human beings with faces and personalities they must be dealt with as people under trying circumstances. You may stop the game whenever your actors fall short of their obligations. When you do so, be sure to discuss what went wrong and lead your actors to tactics and choices that will get them back on track.

Take, for example, the moment of the first killing. In earlier rounds, it may have taken some time for all players to realize and deal with the fact that someone has died. Dialogue and given circumstances require that in this improvisation, everyone will immediately realize that a death has occurred and will have to deal with this fact as a group activity. Your actors will have to make choices that are consistent with reality. What would be done if someone dropped over at a party? One or more guests might call for medical aid. Finding and using a phone would then become an issue. As host, you may have to reenter the scene to keep the plot contained within the room. Perhaps you have removed all phones before your guests entered, or perhaps no phones are working. For your actors, a failure to find a phone must be handled as a new discovery and as an obstacle that must be overcome. As the second body drops to the floor, the communal discovery and growing dread must be played out. Each time a new discovery is made, a heightened set of stakes must affect the choices enacted by your students.

Your murderer, on the other hand, will have dialogue and given circumstances to hide behind while playing out his objective. In the improvisation, the murderer has the ability to seem like part of the group and use that facade to find opportunities to kill. A murderer might choose to blend into the crowd; another might shy away; and still another might become a leader in the unfolding social dynamic. At any rate, what players say and do will be judged by the other actors and the audience watching, so the murderer will have wonderful opportunities to develop a throughline of action.

The important development here is that the game has become secondary to the story unfolding on the stage. The game will now be only a device to give your students the opportunity to do all the things that actors would have to do if this were a scene from a play, rather than an acting exercise. Whether the dialogue is provided by a script or improvised, as it is in this exercise, actors will be required to make choices consistent with the logic and power of the unfolding story. The given circumstances, reactions to the big plot events, and tactical choices demanded by the life-and-death situation at hand will have to be acknowledged and handled by your actors.

Wrap-up

Good actors know the story they are a part of. They learn to recognize the throughline of action of the overall story and their part in that story. They also know that by identifying the conflict in any particular story, they can determine an objective to play that will serve the unfolding story. They can further delineate the tactics they will use by analyzing the given circumstances and by asking themselves the "magic if." They will respond to and make mileage out of victories, defeats, discoveries, and new information while making choices that are as exciting as the situation and the characters they are playing will allow. And they will do all this while responding in the moment. Murder! gives student actors the opportunity to recognize and develop all these necessary actor skills without having to deal with a script.

Listening and Working Moment to Moment

Did you ever notice that when your students do an improv, they have an uncanny ability to listen to each other? Their skill at playing off fellow actors is often marvelous. They can pick up on each others' thoughts and actions as easily as Desmond Morris can read body language. Situations are created and developed as fast as suburban Levittowns after World War II. And yet, when these same students are asked to do a reading from a script, they seem almost oblivious that other actors are even there, let alone try to create an interactive scene. When one of these actors delivers a line to the other, no matter how loaded with important new information or plot-turning dramatic possibility, the other responds with the prescribed dialogue as if what was just said was no more than empty chatter. Literally, no dramatic moments are discovered or played out by the actors. The acting is done in a vacuum, and the scene turns out fuzzy, dull, and totally devoid of dramatic movement.

This same acting disease often infects high school productions. The cast of the typical high school play, though a few actors may deliver captivating performances, often demonstrates little outstanding acting if we objectively judge what we see. It is seldom a matter of talent, however. Many of these same students later graduate from college programs as solid actors. No doubt they have learned some craft during their college training that has helped amplify their natural talent. But, in many cases, the most significant change an audience sees in their work is the use of a stage technique that they naturally used during improv: they have learned to listen.

Too often, when a high school actor turns on the charisma in a production, what we get is a performance—as defined by Webster, someone who "gives a public presentation or exhibition." The performer repeats that performance over and over again exactly the same way regardless of what else may be happening onstage. But is it believable? If the performance takes place in a vacuum—without paying attention to the intrinsic dramatic story elements and without acknowledging what happened onstage the moment before or that the other actors are making choices and completing actions—that glitzy performance will never evolve into great acting.

Again and again, I find myself telling auditioning high school actors who bring in realistic material that "I like their performance." Then I find myself telling them that no one passing by would have mistaken their work for real life. This is ironic in a way, since the vast majority of today's young actors have been far more influenced by film and television acting than by the stage. In film, moment-to-moment believability is essential, and even an untrained audience can smell the difference. So why, when we see a high school play, does an audience pretend that an energized but totally unbelievable performance, a performance without moments of discovery, victory, and defeat, is perfectly wonderful? Why does the drama teacher directing the high school play settle for an energized performance, when it might be possible to have good acting too?

No doubt part of the reason is time. There just isn't enough of it to get that play up on its feet by the production date. When the high school director sees a kid putting out that performance energy, he knows that actor will carry the material well enough to keep the audience entertained. Rather than messing with a formula that seems to be working, the director moves on to the bigger problems that are facing him as opening day approaches. But there are two sides to the acting quotient. First, an actor must serve the script and production by telling the story simply, cleanly, and dramatically. Second, he must be able to do so with believability intact. One side without the other will never produce great acting or, at least with realistic material, never produce a completely satisfying production.

All, right then, what can be done to help your young actors listen and interact better onstage? The first thing you can do is to take the time in rehearsals to ensure that your actors really are listening to each other. Often they are not. Interrupt them during a scene and ask them what another actor has just said to them. Ask them what the comment meant. In life, when people speak to us, we can usually repeat verbatim what has just been said to us. We can almost always interpret what we have just been told for subtext, for nuance, for connotation. We can do this because we are sensitive to tone, rhythm, body language, and a host of other indicators that all come under the category of listening. We do this automatically. Its part of our built-in system of communications. When actors don't do this stuff, it is usually a result of not paying attention to the speaker. When that happens, believability is a lost cause.

So if the actor is not listening, what is he doing? In most cases the actor is waiting to say his next line, oblivious to both what is being said and the manner in which it is delivered. He is focused on himself. But unless the inspiration for that next line is clearly heard by that actor, the spoken line will never have more meaning than the line itself possesses. If that is all the audience gets, they might as well be reading the play at home and save the price of admission. A good imagination can provide more excitement than a nonlistening actor can.

If you teach your actors in class as well as in rehearsals, try playing some repetition games with them. You might try saying something as simple as "I love you" to your students. Say it to each of them, one at a time, and make them say it back to you.

Their response should reflect the way you said it to them. If your "I love you" is passionate, they need to take that in. If it is paternal, their response should somehow reflect that fact. Every return should somehow play off the transmitted message. There are thousands of ways to say "I love you," and each one conveys a particular meaning. Each response must actively reflect what has been taken in by the listener. Your students will no doubt discover that listening provides them with a palette of colors they did not dream they possessed.

Make a long list of emotionally charged key phrases that you can say to your students, or get them to help you make the list. Then, go through the list with them using the same process described above. If the response does not reflect the initiating statement, repeat it for the student again and again until you get an appropriate response. A statement will only be charged if it carries new and interesting information that requires the receiving actor to take it in and deal with it before a response can be made.

Sanford Meisner, one of the great first-generation American acting teachers that sprang from the Group Theater, spent a good part of his teaching career developing and working with a series of sequential repetition games. Meisner strongly believed that listening and being in the moment were two of the most important attributes of good acting. If you are not familiar with his work or are interested in trying his sequence of repetition games with your students, you might check out *Sanford Meisner on Acting* by Sanford Meisner and Dennis Longwell or *The Sanford Meisner Approach* by Larry Silverberg. Both will provide you with ample material to begin to get your students listening to each other onstage.

If your time with your actors is limited to rehearsals, make the best use of that time by making sure your actors are always playing objectives. Make it clear to them that they must be fully aware of what they are doing as well as feeling during every moment onstage. If their objectives are connected with the actors who are sharing the stage with them at any particular time (and they should be), then your actors will certainly have to tune into each other. They can't get what they need in the scene from the other actors if they don't. It is not unusual for directors to describe the results they are looking for—and for trained actors, this poses no problem. A skilled actor can usually translate result-oriented directions into doable actions without help. But student actors often cannot. If you take the time to talk actions and objectives to your students, you will find that you have gone a long way toward preventing those "performances in a vacuum." In the long run, you will probably save time in rehearsal as well. If your students understand what they are doing in a scene, they will be better able to make choices for themselves that work. The result is you will be able to spend more time fixing and creating where your production most needs it.

Instant Playwriting

I use this exercise to point out how important good listening onstage can be. It convincingly makes clear that playing strong, simple objectives onstage will result in strong, clear, and compelling acting. Furthermore, the exercise makes a granite hard case for the interconnectedness of listening and objective playing. Surprisingly then, the exercise, at least in the early stages, is played without any spoken dialogue. All listening is done with the eyes—because all verbal communication is done with the written word.

Method

Ask your students to select a strong objective that can be obtained from someone else in the class. Suggest to your students that they use the verb phrase *to make* to state their objective, as in "to make her . . ." This verb phrase guarantees that the objective selected will be a strong one. The *her* reference guarantees that the objective can only be obtained by engaging a scene partner. Have your students write their objectives down to ensure that they have been specific with themselves. A written objective might say "to make someone feel better," or "to make someone help me," or even "to make someone kiss me." Leave it up to them. If they have picked a weak objective, they will soon learn experientially the importance of going into a scene armed with a stronger one.

Once everyone has a strong objective to play, your class should pair off. If there is an odd number and there has to be a group of three, it will be harder for that group to have a successful exercise, just as it is harder for a playwright to effectively write a multicharacter scene than it is to write for two characters. It might be a better idea to have one student play two separate exercises at the same time. Try it both ways and see for yourself.

The process of the exercise is simple. One student in each group writes a first line of dialogue on a piece of paper. His partner should not be able to see what is being written. The written dialogue should be a first step toward obtaining the stated objective. Only when the piece of dialogue is completed should it be handed to the student's partner. When the first line of dialogue has been read by the second, she will respond in writing to the dialogue, while at the same time trying to pursue her own objective. However, there is now an obstacle for the second actor. She cannot pursue her objective without acknowledging what the first writer has put on the table through his dialogue. In other words, her dialogue must somehow acknowledge what is now on the table. She must try to redirect the conversation to find a way back to her objective, but if her response is to be believable, she must now incorporate whatever has just been said. Suddenly the actor realizes that strategy will be necessary if her objective is to be obtained. Each new piece of dialogue should be short. The purpose of the game will be destroyed if the players write long monologues for themselves in an effort to redirect the flow of dialogue. When my students play the game, I allow them to write only one sentence at a time, at least at first.

DISCUSSION

Even in the early stages of the exercise you will begin to hear spontaneous emotional responses to the material your students are reading. You will also observe that each pair of actors will go through a similar process during and after the reading of each newly delivered line. In the first stage, they will read the delivered line in the same manner they would hear the line spoken in an acting situation. Then they will react to that line. Finally they will initiate a response by writing the new line of dialogue. This will happen clearly and fully with each new line introduced.

In no time at all, it will become clear to you that your student are connected to the material more strongly than you have ever seen them be with scripted material that is not already well rehearsed. Your students will notice the difference as well. Each new piece of information, each new discovery, each little victory and defeat will be registered and played by your actors. The freedom they feel and the spontaneity they project will fuel them in ways you would not have thought possible. Since there is no written dialogue beyond what they are writing in the moment, they cannot be distracted by anticipating or by thinking about their own next line—that is, until they themselves make it up. Because they are truly in each moment, your students will be able to react with a level of spontaneity usually reserved for real life. The lesson about listening onstage becomes eminently clear.

Furthermore, because they will be pursuing specific objectives through the use of dialogue they themselves make up, your students' ability to stay focused on these objectives will noticeably increase. As a result, each pair of students will probably find a reason for conflict quickly, and the improvisational dialogue will quickly take on the dramatic qualities that a written scene possesses. There will be clear-cut beats, transitions, and an ongoing throughline of conflict that leads directly toward a well-earned fulfilling climax.

Once an Instant Playwriting scene has been completed—and your students will probably be able to make that conclusion themselves—give them a couple of minutes to rehearse the scene they have written. Then have them read it with each other to the class. In most cases you will find that your students demonstrate a fairly good retention level for what they discovered while playing the exercise. They are usually able to play more fully and with more legitimate moments than their typical scene-reading work possesses. Their reading will usually seem more spontaneous and natural as well.

The lessons regarding listening are, for the most part, quite obvious, and your students should have no trouble making the connection between the exercise and their own scripted work. The connection between the impromptu script they have created, however, and a script written by a good playwright is probably less apparent. In good dramatic writing, the playwright has written only what is absolutely necessary to tell the story. If something doesn't serve a specific purpose, a good playwright will omit it. In most cases a playwright is intentionally creating and developing conflict at all times because she is interested in making a compelling story for the stage. Consciously or not, she is pitting one character against another in her work, and for the actor, this translates into opposing objectives.

In the exercise, your actors will have created their own objectives, and because they know what they are, they will be able to play them clearly and fully. The feeling of freedom and spontaneity they will experience will stay with them for a while. They will be motivated to re-create this feeling with their scripted assignments as well. Your students will eventually be able to do so if they can learn to translate the conflict their scene work contains into playable objectives. That skill will be mastered sooner—if they develop their abilities to listen to their partners and stay in the moment.

I sometimes have my students play the first round of this exercise without telling them to choose an objective. This omission usually results in some interesting and funny moment-to-moment beats of dialogue, but few pairings are able to create a situation that can be fully developed because there is no built-in source of conflict that objectives provide. A discussion about this can provide a natural segue into playing the game again with objectives. If you play additional rounds, you might ask your students to establish some given circumstances beforehand. Doing so will lay the groundwork for an even more specific scene creation. It might even lead to a spontaneous, but nonetheless, brilliant play. Who knows?

The Mirror Game

The Mirror Game, like doing the balcony scene from *Romeo and Juliet* or Nina's—"I am seagull" scene from *The Seagull* by Chekhov, is an acting-class rite of passage. No self-respecting actors can say they have had acting training without having played it at least once or, even more likely, at least once per teacher. But The Mirror Game, more than most standard introductory theater games used in acting classes, seems to confound its players as to its real purpose and meaning. Only when I began using the game in my own classes did its true value become clear for me; and it was only after it had, that I began to emphasize its essential actor significance in a way that my students could understand. Once that happened, the game's purpose began having the impact on my students that I desired.

I was reminded again just recently of the importance of the game and how difficult it is to do successfully. I had already completed a series of partnering exercises during a recruiting workshop when I got to The Mirror Game. High school students of varying ages, talent, and training had been participating in my workshop bringing, for the most part, an unbridled Saturday morning enthusiasm. When I announced we would be playing The Mirror Game, there was a mix of knowing head bobs and blank looks. But after I explained the game and allowed my workshop students to begin playing, any seeming differences between the veterans in the game and the novices quickly disappeared. In general, they all played with the same intensity and glee, and most completely missed the point of the game—in spite of the fact that I had emphasized its purpose and significance during my introduction. Once again, it hit me: the difficulty in getting young actors to understand the importance of connecting with their partners and the importance of training them to be able to do so. That, of course, is the essence of what The Mirror Game should be about.

Purpose

The Mirror Game requires students to focus completely on their partners. Their concentration is, therefore, entirely external. To meet the obligations of the game, the players must be completely in tune with their partners, observing and instantaneously copying whatever they see their partners doing. Each movement must be executed in such a way that it can be copied almost instantaneously. This requires teamwork and connection between the participants that cannot be achieved unless the partners are truly working as a unit. This is the metaphor for good acting—as the game should make clear.

To achieve the simultaneous effect that is the goal of the game, the players must sacrifice their desire to be in control and replace it with a willingness to be in the moment instead. That can happen only when all senses are tuned in to the other player and, obviously, off themselves. Each pairing must find a way to allow that to happen. When partners find that way, they have discovered the magic that this kind of spontaneity onstage can bring. It is our obligation as teachers to make sure that this message not only gets across to our students during the exercise but also that our students have the vital experience of connection during their mirror play.

The Mirror Game offers several other learning opportunities. Given enough time to explore the game's possibilities, students will learn or learn about the following:

- to use their bodies in ways they might not ordinarily use them

- to develop their eye-body coordination

- to develop their ability to use and relate to space and height

- to begin to see the ways that proximity or distance can affect the work of actors onstage

- to develop their sensitivity to pace and tempo and its effect on communication

- to develop their physical vocabulary with regard to gesture and physical action

- to discover the power of risk taking

- to develop their risk-taking skills without sacrificing the vital stage partnership

The Mirror Game also provides students with the opportunity of experiencing how spontaneous emotion can be generated when an actor is freed from self-consciousness by focusing outside the self. Few other acting games produce the level of concentration and resulting gleeful emotion that The Mirror Game can provide when played with the proper mind-set and attitude.

Method
ROUND 1
The game is very simple to play; it is just difficult to play well. But, like riding a bicycle, once the basic principle is mastered, the players can focus on the scenery rather than the mechanics. The first step is to divide your class into pairs. Each pair should face each other, two to three feet apart. They should stand in a neutral position with arms at their sides. Give them time to simply look at each other until they become comfortable. At first this may not be easy for them. Self-consciousness is likely to cause them to giggle or to wiggle or rock or to look everywhere but directly at their partners. Folded or awkward arms and hands are not unusual either. When you observe these physicalizations, remind students to make adjustments.

A bit of patience and some positive coaching may be necessary to get your students to settle into the all-important task of actually looking at each other. Don't proceed until the pairings are able to do so. If there are pairings that, even after patient coaching, won't settle into the required behavior, either ask them to sit down and watch until they can get control over themselves, or try re-pairing several partnerships. It might be wise to monitor the pairings beforehand to prevent potentially troublesome partnerships.

Once your students are able to look at each other without resorting to self-conscious behavior, they are ready to hear the rules of the exercise. Allow them to continue looking at each other while you tell them the following:

> The mirror game is intended to force you to connect with your partner. Your objective is to get totally in synch with each other so that someone watching cannot tell which of you is initiating the movement and which of you is copying or reflecting the movement of the initiator like a mirror. No one wins or loses in this game. Your purpose is simply to find a way to work together completely. Therefore, it is the obligation of the initiator to make movements that can be copied simultaneously, and it is the obligation of the reflector to observe, as closely as possible, what the initiator is doing. If someone observing can tell who is leading, then you have not done your job properly. What you want to do is to find a way of creating the illusion of absolute simultaneous action.

You can, if you want, assign the roles of leader and follower, but it really doesn't matter in the long run. Once the directions are understood, give the go-ahead to begin playing and see what happens. If, by the way, during your direction giving, some of your students begin looking at you rather than at their partners, return their focus to their partners. Also remind them of any returning nervous physical movements. These reminders will make them aware that their bodies reflect their own inner feelings—a liability when trying to portray a character that does not necessarily share those feelings. Also repeat for your students that the purpose of the game is to stay connected with their partners in spite of what may be going on elsewhere. If you assign the initiators, the game will crank up immediately. If you tell your players to just see what happens, one of each pair will probably begin initiating rather than face the unknown. If no one takes the initiative in a particular pairing, it won't be long before a leader establishes herself. Have no fear about that.

When the players begin, you will observe a wide variety of styles and technique. Those who have played before will probably rely on hand and arm movements only. Their physicalization will probably resemble an Eastern Tai-chi-like exercise, but even the experienced students will probably take a little time before they can establish a tempo that allows their partners to keep up with them. The beginners will likely have a terrible time. The novice initiator will probably move much too fast and do far too many movements for the reflector to follow. This may lead to a loss of concentration and laughter, or it may simply reveal students that are so oblivious to the moment that they keep right on going in spite of the fact that they have left their partners far behind.

After a reasonable amount of time has elapsed, during which the players should have established a rhythm for working together, you might try coaching a bit. Remind students about the purpose of the game, suggest that they slow down the tempo if they are having trouble staying together, and offer clues for adjusting their visual focus to stay in synch with their partners. Also remind the students having the most difficulty with concentration that until they are able to discipline themselves and focus on their objective, there will be little hope of mastering the fine points of the game. When you are satisfied that your pairings have gotten the most they can from each other, tell them to reverse roles and try again. They will probably do better this time since they have already viewed the game from their partner's perspective.

Round 2

Once you are satisfied that things are going well, ask your students to switch partners. They will quickly discover that a new partner means a new set of dynamics, a new way of working, and a new set of problems to solve. You might comment about this as the new pairings are trying to establish their new relationship. You could also point out that what they are experiencing is no different than when two new scene partners begin working together. The acting dynamics between partners in scene work is always new each time a fresh partnership is begun.

It is part of the acting obligation to find the most effective way to relate to a scene partner to accomplish the goals of the scene. Different actors playing the same role always bring different characteristics and choices to the work. An actor who does not adjust to this new input fails in her acting responsibility. Actors must always be as conscious of the new moment as they are to their overall objectives. All the homework and planning an actor does must be distilled through the events that happen spontaneously on the stage. Actors who fail to adjust to the moment never attain the highest level of work, work that results in surprising choices that come from listening and adjusting to the special circumstances created each time a moment is played out. The emotional reactions your students exhibit as they play The Mirror Game comes from this very phenomenon.

Round 3

When the time seems right, ask your students to switch partners again and repeat the procedure. After a few more changes, you should notice that most of your students have now become more skillful and economical about establishing a relationship and a way of working. At this point, you might tell your students that they can change initiators and reflectors at will. In other words, it will now be up to them, without discussion, to change who is the leader and who is the follower. At first your students may balk at this idea because they won't know how a smooth transition of leadership can be accomplished. They may even ask you for an explanation. Simply tell them to figure it out as they work. Before long they will have found a way to do so, and more important, will be totally enthralled that the switch happens so easily and with such fulfilling emotional results. At this point, they will be experiencing the full magic of truly working together. They will be totally in tune with each other, listening with all their senses, focused totally on their partners rather than themselves. In short, they will be living in the moment.

ROUND 4
Now that your students are riding their bikes with ease, you can begin adding some challenges. Suggest to your students that they begin to use height and space as part of their mirroring activities. They can bend and stretch, use the floor, work in profile, and a host of other things. The more adventurous members of your group have probably already begun to do this. You can also suggest that your students begin to use space. They can move toward or away from each other; they can move laterally, diagonally, or even in circles.

The only rule that they can't violate is the rule that makes everything they do possible: They must stay visually focused with each other, or the simultaneous illusion becomes impossible. Some students will, of course, forget this obvious fact because the new possibilities of the game are so engaging and challenging. But the players will soon develop a vocabulary of what works and what doesn't. They will realize that proximity and distance affects focus and perspective. They will learn to adjust. They will also develop a set of standards with regard to speed and tempo that keeps the game going smoothly.

At this point you will probably notice that your class is responding quite regularly with sound—mostly gleeful. This phenomenon happens because your students are now playing so well together and are so focused on their partners, rather than on themselves, that spontaneous emotional responses occur. In actor lingo, they are playing their objectives, the success of which always resides with their acting partners, and they are totally focused on their needs rather than their feelings. Because of this, self-consciousness has, for the most part, disappeared. Further, the more challenging the physicalization, the more concentration required; the more concentration required, the less self-editing produced; the less self-editing produced, the more opportunity to react with genuine emotional spontaneity.

Once your students are moving across the floor and exploring space, they are pretty much in control of the game. Your job then becomes more of a recorder of the good, the interesting, and the discussable. Mentally record or write down worthwhile observations for class discussion and reinforcement later on. Of course, every so often you should call for a change of partners to keep things interesting. The more your students play, the easier all this becomes, of course, and the more sophisticated and free the movements will become. You will start seeing students move in ways and with a freedom that you never dreamed you'd be seeing. Be sure to share with your students the kinds of changes you saw in their physical behavior, and encourage your students to try to maintain this kind of physical freedom when they go back to their scripted acting work. Also, keep reminding them that the changes they exhibited primarily resulted from the freedom that focusing on external tasks can bring.

LATER ROUNDS

Once your students have become masters of the basic Mirror Game, you can introduce them to a set of variations that have evolved from my own work with the game. It has been my observation in recent years that, more and more, students act only from their necks up. Their ability to use their bodies seems to have, in general, become increasingly limited. The variations suggested below might begin to open up your students to a broader vocabulary of physical choices. At the least, your students are likely to discover how much fun using their bodies in an imaginative way can be.

On the following page is a list of themes that that your students can use while playing the game. Hopefully, these themes can provide the impetus for inspired movement and gesture. While your students are playing The Mirror Game, simply call out the name of the theme and see what your students come up with. You might say, for instance, "Samurai Mirror!" and expect that your students will come up with movement that indeed suggests Japanese samurai movement, either of the Kurosawa or John Belushi variety. It doesn't really matter. What is important is that your students are outside themselves, focused on their partners, and coming up with physical actions that are totally foreign to their ordinary physical vocabulary. Use your imagination when reading the following list and think about what these movements might consist of. Add your own variations as you think them up, now, or as they cross your mind while your class is actually engaged in the exercise.

MIRROR GAME THEMES

Ballet mirror game

Opera diva mirror game

Clown mirror game

Cowboy mirror game

Marching band mirror game

Marionette mirror game

Rag doll mirror game

Foreign movie mirror game

Monster mirror game

Frankenstein mirror game

Rock star mirror game

Conductor mirror game

Three Stooges mirror game

The Audio Mirror Game

Finally, here is a variation that was inspired by one of the many torment games my brother and I engaged in while we were kids. Maybe you did this one too. It is played in the same manner as the regular mirror game, except the reflector tries to copy what the initiator is saying simultaneously: as the initiator speaks, the reflector tries to say exactly what the initiator is saying even as the initiator says it. Again, this variation requires a tremendous amount of working together and a commitment to the partner rather than to the self.

For the game to work, the initiator must, at least at first, speak slowly enough for the reflector to keep up. It is not unusual for the initiator to elongate words, especially the vowels, to clue his partner into what he is going to say. The reflector can begin to anticipate where the sentence is going, based on what she has heard already, as long as the initiator doesn't purposely throw curveballs at his partner. Curveballs will be thrown, of course, in the early innings, but when they are, just remind your students that the purpose of the game is to work together.

Once your students begin to get the hang of this variation, the emotional effect is even more intense than a well-played regular mirror game. The listening required in this one is so demanding that spontaneous emotional reactions are almost impossible to avoid. You will find that even your most stoic student will be pulled into the immediacy of The Audio Mirror Game. Further, you will find a commensurate use of physical gestures even though this is the audio version of the game. The heightened emotions, along with concentrated listening, seem to demand an engagement of the body. By the time your students are in high gear, you will marvel at the physical and emotional results.

Wrap-up

In conclusion, The Mirror Game allows students to experience the acting potential that working closely together with a partner can bring. It allows them, like an actor in a scene, to focus on task and objective. It requires them to make all choices dependent on what their partner is doing. It requires them to observe and stay connected with their partners at all times with all their senses. Finally, it allows student actors to experience the emotional effects of throwing their focus away from themselves and onto purpose, when that purpose resides in the actors sharing the stage with them.

No wonder The Mirror Game is an acting-class rite of passage.

Russian Roulette

There are about half a dozen films that I have seen that have so profoundly affected me emotionally that I consider them autobiographical events. Not all these films are among the best I have ever seen, but there was something about each of them that reached straight into my affective domain, bypassing my intellect completely.

One of these films, *The Deer Hunter*, was the first to deal with the emotional ravages of the Vietnam War in a realistic way. Since I am of that era, the wounds exhibited by the characters touched me with their familiarity and explicitness. But I was also struck by the games of Russian Roulette played in the film.

Though film critics might cite only the metaphorical nature of the game, the several Russian Roulette sequences, brought to life by director Michael Cimino and his talented cast, were, for me, some of the most dramatically riveting sequences I have ever seen on film. Whenever I think about those scenes, my body tightens up. My mind zeros in on close-up images of Robert De Niro, John Savage, and Christopher Walken, who played the game in several scenes—their faces as clear as if I had just walked out of the theater that first time.

In the film, De Niro and his men are captured by a band of Vietcong renegades who play Russian Roulette to pass the time. Their captors force them to play, the Vietcong chief threatening to kill them if they don't. To protect his troops from certain death, De Niro verbally attacks the young and recalcitrant John Savage to get him to play. Because the audience understands the goodness underlying De Niro's seeming cruelty, the exchange has unforgettable power.

The game they play creates as much tension, moment for moment, as any movie sequence I have seen. Each second is filled with the time-stopping power of life and death. I can still remember the spell-like silence that befell the audience all three times I saw the film on screen. The audience literally stopped breathing, together as one, each time the gun barrel was put to someone's temple, and the sighs of relief after the trigger came down on an empty chamber seemed orchestrated. I can remember hearing my heartbeats during each repetition of the life-and-death dance, and the literal exhaustion I felt when that first roulette game was finally over.

Some of the best acting I have ever seen on film occurred during this sequence and during the Russian Roulette betting sequences later in the film. Christopher Walken went on to win an Academy Award for his supporting role as the guy who became obsessed with the druglike power of the game, and his transition during the film from warm, caring human being to zombie is unforgettable.

Purpose

It was Christopher Walken's performance that made me realize Russian Roulette's potential as an acting exercise. The game provided Walken with a life-and-death struggle, which enabled him to demonstrate his acting chops. It struck me that using Russian Roulette as part of the given circumstances of an acting exercise could do the same for a group of acting students.

The two principal characteristics that define good acting are believability and telling the best possible story. Most actors who get work manage, at least on screen, to accomplish the former; but the second, telling the best possible story, is often ignored completely. Generally speaking, when actors make small but believable choices, it is the material that gets blamed: the script is boring, not the actor. But there is no doubt that when an actor makes choices that are both believable and carry the weight of life and death, they will get noticed, and the notice will be positive. The life-and-death stakes of Russian Roulette in *The Deer Hunter* make this clear. Christopher Walken has never been better on screen.

Using Russian Roulette as an acting exercise can do the same for your students in class. All the elements of drama are built right into Russian Roulette. The stakes could not be higher. The basic premise of the game forces even the most retiring students to make big choices. Tremendous obstacles are also built in. Each player must overcome his own fears to complete the requirements of the game. Also built into the exercise is a strong and simple objective: Each player certainly wants to win, for losing means dying.

But even more important, a simulation of Russian Roulette forces each player to pay attention and respond at every moment. Each moment is critical, because it could be the players' last. Participants are forced to take in every moment and respond to it with specific choices that clarify their thoughts and feelings. The game provides a compelling arena for acting that is believable and tells an exceptionally strong story.

Method

In Russian Roulette, a single cartridge is loaded in a revolver with a six-chamber cylinder: Five chambers remain empty; one contains the mechanism of death. The cylinder is spun like the wheel of fortune so that the contestants do not know where the deadly cartridge lies. Each contestant takes a turn with the revolver, squeezing off a single shot. The game continues until a contestant pulls the trigger on the chamber containing the cartridge. Then the game is over.

Over the years, I have come up with several possible variations of the exercise. If you try the game in your own class, no doubt you will come up with several more. The game can be adapted for variations in the age and size of your class and amount of time you wish to spend using the concept. Before we begin, however, we should probably talk about the gun.

For years I used a metal cap gun. It looked fairly real, but once held, it clearly felt like a toy. I often use guns in acting exercises not because I approve of them in any way—I don't—but as an acting device, I find that the more real the prop, the easier it is for the student to commit to the reality of the situation. A gun, by its nature, creates a life-and-death situation, and acting with high stakes is critically important to an actor's craft. Today in my college acting classes, I use an air pistol that has the look and feel of a real gun. It's amazing how much easier my students make the jump once they feel the prop's heft and metal coldness. But rest assured, the game can be played with a plastic water pistol, a cap gun, or just a hand held in the gun position. The point of the exercise is about making moments.

Obviously, this game may not be appropriate for some high school classes, or you yourself might not be comfortable using this game. High Stakes Poker, an alternative described later in this chapter, may be more appropriate for you and your class. But even if you choose not to use this variation of Russian Roulette, the acting concepts discussed here should prove valuable to you and your students.

THE IMPROVISATIONAL EXERCISE

This version requires no preparation for the class. Without any introductory instruction, ask your students to sit in a wide circle. When they are seated, tell them that the acting exercise is about to begin and that they are to react to your instructions without asking for background information. They must accept the simple instructions and pretend to believe in the reality simply because it is required. At this point, pull out the gun and tell them they are going to play Russian Roulette. Explain the game. Be sure to insert the pretend cartridge and spin the cylinder. Then place the gun in the center of the circle.

You can start the game by assigning someone to go first, or

you can wait for someone to pick up the gun. You can also assume the role of antagonist and threaten the group until someone does pick up the gun. Once the first person has played the game, you can wait for another volunteer, or you can tell the group to proceed in a clockwise direction. The game continues until everyone has had a turn, or until one of your students has pulled the trigger on a loaded chamber. Simply put, that is the process. You may stop the exercise to comment on the work at any time you feel that it is necessary.

DISCUSSION

If you are uncomfortable with the idea of someone actually putting a bullet into her head, even in a pretend situation, you can instruct the class that when the time is right, you will inform them who will get the loaded chamber. Or you can simply not allow the loaded chamber ever to be fired by making that part of the rules. The most important acting element for the class is playing the potential stakes moment by moment.

Russian Roulette requires players to respond continuously because each moment provides new life-and-death information that is dramatically interesting and because practically each moment demands a response. Even the instructions are filled with dramatic potential. By using the "magic if" (what would I do if I were in this situation?), your students can provide themselves with an arsenal of acting choices. What would they do when informed they will be playing Russian Roulette? When they see the cartridge loaded and the chamber spun? What would they do while sitting next to the person about to fire? How would they connect with each other at every moment? How would the group experience influence their individual game playing?

As each player takes his turn, he has the opportunity to perform a sequence of actions with a beginning, middle, and end. The knowledge that the stakes are ultimate informs each action. First, the actor realizes it is finally his turn to test his fate. Then he decides to pick up the gun and put it against his head. Deciding to squeeze the trigger comes next. Finally, the biggest moment—squeezing the trigger on an empty chamber and post-poning death—offers up wonderful acting possibilities. Each action defines a life-and-death sequence that carries enormous dramatic potential because the stakes could not be higher. As each actor takes his turn, the others must watch and react, mostly with empathy: first, because they realize their own turn is coming, and second, because the anticipation of impending tragedy hangs on every moment.

The most important acting concept to emphasize in this round of the game is the necessity of taking in and reacting to each dramatic moment as it comes up. The group situation also emphasizes the importance of taking in the group's reaction as well as creating one in isolation. Keep in mind that playing the situation is as important as following the rules of the game, so be prepared to analyze and praise reactions that are believable but not necessarily what you expected.

For instance, a student who plays her objective to survive by turning the gun on you, although taking liberties with the rules, has found a strong action to play, one that is dramatic and believable. The student who runs for the door rather than follow your instructions is also playing the situation extremely well. Once those choices have been played out, you can create given circumstances that no longer permit such choices. You could inform the students that the door is locked or that your gun is fixed on them, in case they want to try any monkey business. Be sure to pay attention to the "magic if": Only allow choices that make sense and are believable.

The students should be able to create a cohesive story line consisting of their individual turns. The reactions to each player's efforts by the rest of the players as individuals and a group can make a compelling improvisation, one that could be repeated and improved upon with each redoing. Remind your students that each person's turn should build dramatically on previous turns. Otherwise, the plotline will remain static, and in a high stakes situation, that would be dramatically unforgivable.

Finally, there is no need for the gun to ever fire if that rule is built into the instructions. If you don't boycott the firing of the gun, however, one of your students may choose, on his own, to pull the trigger on the loaded chamber and die. If that happens, don't forget to spend some time discussing that dying onstage provides the actor with an opportunity to shape a dramatic sequence. For many actors, dying onstage is a fabulous acting opportunity, too good to ruin by not putting any thought into it.

THE PREPARED EXERCISE

For this prepared assignment, students will be responsible for creating and carrying out a story in which the central action is Russian Roulette.

1. Create the given circumstances for playing Russian Roulette (who, what, when, where).
2. Provide the motivation for playing game. Make sure there is justification and logic to the situation.
3. Determine the relationship between the players.
4. Through improvisation, create a script in which the characters created engage in a game of Russian Roulette. Make sure your script includes the following:
   - a plot with a beginning, middle, and end that builds to a climax
   - moment-to-moment reactions to all new information
   - life-and-death stakes
   - big choices
   - a script that has the game played out to the sixth and final chamber
5. Rehearse and perform your script in class.

The class should be given whatever you feel is an appropriate amount of time in or out of class to prepare this exercise. In all probability, the prepared scene will contain some problems regarding clarity, believability, and logical progression, to name a few. After the scene is shown, discuss its merits and flaws with the actors and the rest of the class. Together, look for ways of solving the problems, and make sure your actors write down important criticisms and suggestions. Allow each team of actors to rethink and rehearse their work in preparation for a second presentation. When the rehearsal period is over, your actors should perform their work for the class once again.

Justifying the reason for the game so that the audience will accept it as believable is one of the most difficult aspects of the exercise, but it is also one of the most rewarding in terms of teaching. When well done, the justification allows your students to look at a tragedy from the inside, and often they develop an empathy and understanding that might never occur to them from reading a newspaper article or hearing a news item on TV. Some of the most successful scenarios I have seen involved teenagers trapped by trying to be cool, preteens finding Dad's gun and playing with it, terminally ill people looking for a way to end their suffering, and macho adults stupidly trying to out-dare each other. Each scenario allows students to examine human behavior from a point of view they might not otherwise consider. The broader educational amplifications are obvious.

High Stakes Poker

The acting concepts brought out in Russian Roulette can be paralleled effectively by substituting the gambling game of straight poker. As long as the stakes are really high, your students will have the opportunity to make those same big choices moment by moment that were available to them in the game with the gun. In the improvisational version, you might begin by using real cards and allowing the students to react to what they are dealt. Once the basics have been mastered, your students can play with imaginary cards, identifying them as they pretend to flip them over. Your students will, however, have to remember the imaginary cards. This is no easy task unless they are very connected with the improvisation, and that, of course, is the point. If the rules of poker are fuzzy for you, just ask your class; they'll quickly refresh your memory. Later, you can add in the high-stakes gambling aspects.

The more at risk, the better. Establish given circumstances that will make the money particularly important. The money could be for a mortgage, or an operation, or to pay kidnappers threatening to murder a kidnapped child. A game of strip poker could provide sufficient high stakes. Or instead of money, your students could bet body parts, as I once saw in an episode of "Tales from the Crypt." Let your students use their imaginations, but make sure all choices are justified and logical.

The most important points are high stakes, playing the moments, logical choices that are believable, and building the tension in the story. Remember, this exercise is intended to develop concepts and tools of acting, so improvement is far more important than product.

THE PREPARED EXERCISE

Play out a hand of poker in which the consequences of losing are terrifying and the possible winnings are extremely high. The drama should continue to build as the betting increases and each new card is laid down. This game has all the elements of drama built in—life and death, high stakes, and a strong objective. It provides an excellent avenue for an acting exercise.

1. Create the given circumstances for playing a game of cards (who, what, when, where).

2. Provide the motivation for playing the game. Make sure there is justification and logic to the situation.

3. Determine the relationship between the contestants.

4. Through improvisation, create a script in which the characters created engage in a game of poker. Make sure your script includes the following:

   - a plot with a beginning, middle, and end that builds to a climax

- moment-to-moment reactions to all new information
- life-and-death stakes
- big choices
- a script that has the game played out to the end of the hand.

5. Rehearse and perform your script in class.

Using People, Places, and Things

As I have pointed out many times in this book, when students make dramatically effective choices, they become actors who will serve the playwright's script well.

In earlier exercises, we have explored how using given circumstances can help an actor bring into focus the essentials of a dramatic scene. Determining the given circumstances—the who, what, when, and where—of any acting situation helps actors narrow down the infinite number of choices available to them at any given moment onstage. This, in turn, allows them to zero in on the acting obligations they must fulfill.

But to a young or inexperienced actor, even this distilling process may yet leave far too many possibilities to see clearly the best dramatic road to travel on. Now it is time to introduce three more tools—the physical self, relationship, and location— that can help your actors isolate and employ the essentials needed to make their scenes work more effectively and probably deepen the work they will be creating.

Using Props and Your Body to Tell the Story: Acting with the Physical Self

I often hear my conservatory actors discussing the youth-oriented dramatic shows they watch on television, and what they say about the acting on those shows is often very critical indeed. They complain vehemently about the work they see on "Felicity" and "Dawson's Creek" and reserve special venom for the less well-acted shows like "90210." Often it is the writing or the life choices of the characters, rather than the acting itself, that my students find fault with. At other times it is the upspeak delivery or flat vocal choices that grates on my young critics. But I have never heard any of my students complain that they don't believe the physicalization of the actors they are so critical of. In movies and film, as we all know, it is what the actor does rather than what he says that counts. Yet, ironically, many of my own actors have difficulty doing the simplest physical things onstage in a believable manner without a lot of prompting or rehearsing.

In the last several years, I have noticed a significant increase in the number of students who are unable to say lines and do things with their bodies in an integrated way. For some of my actors this results in an inability to deliver lines in a consistently believable manner because they haven't discovered the action that motivates the saying of those lines. These actors find themselves forced into arbitrarily trying to discover a reading that works. They are handicapped because they are acting only from the neck up. For others, this same lack of integration between head and body results in self-sabotage. They destroy believable line readings because their actions are far less convincing than their verbal delivery.

More significantly, I have noticed that an increasing number of students are totally oblivious to the fact that what they do physically during a scene is every bit as important for telling the story as the written dialogue. They fail to understand that physicalization is part of the actor's toolkit and that by consciously choosing effective movements, they can reveal character and carve out wonderful moments in an ongoing throughline. This physical perspective on acting is totally alien to their way of thinking. Fortunately, once they are exposed to thinking in terms of physicalization, they immediately grasp its importance and usefulness. But for many students, it remains hard to choose appropriate physical actions, and for some, it is even harder to execute these choices in a believable manner.

What follows is a sequence of exercises that require students to tell their stories through physical actions. First and foremost, these exercises require students to think about their blocking—their chosen movements onstage, the gestures they use to communicate their stories, and the business, or ongoing activity, they must create to keep their stories believable and clear. Second, by using props, your students will discover that the connection they make between themselves and the props they work with often leads to clearer and more specific and emotionally involved acting.

Hug a Pillow, Slug a Pillow

Purpose

This exercise demonstrates to your student actors that a physical action applied to a prop can both let the audience know what a character onstage is thinking and feeling, and help create those feelings in the actor executing that action. Further, the feelings generated are more believable, more heartfelt, and more connected with the ongoing action than when an actor tries to conjure feeling directly. Your students should also learn that dialogue is not a province of its own, separate from the physical action of a scene, but, rather, a partner to the action, connected by and to it through the given circumstances of the story being told.

Method
ROUND 1

Ask your students to bring in a pillow or stuffed animal from home. The pillow or animal should be on the sturdy side and in good shape. If it's a stuffed animal or pillow that has personal meaning to your actors, all the better. At the time you begin, you may want to go around the room and allow each of your students to describe the relationship they have with the stuffed partner they have brought with them. You might get responses like "It's the pillow I've slept on since I was four" or "This is the stuffed animal my late grandma gave me and I've been sleeping with it since I was a little kid." Once your students are comfortable with their own prop and are comfortable with seeing everyone else with theirs, you are ready to begin.

Ask your students to hug their prop with commitment. Make sure they all fulfill this obligation. It may require, especially for the guys, several attempts. When everyone has fully committed to the activity and is satisfied with what they have done, discuss the results with your class. Expect that several of your students will report surprising reactions.

DISCUSSION

When your students are discussing the history of their pillow or stuffed animal before the first round begins, you may notice a physical connection between your students and their prop as they speak. A way of looking at the object as a student speaks, a particular kind of touching as personal history is revealed, may make clear that there is genuine affection between the speaker and her object. Make your students aware of this phenomenon and have them pay particular attention for telling gestures that clearly express the relationship between the speaker and her inanimate companion. This will help your students come to realize how important physical work can be to their acting.

Once the exercise begins, it should become instantly clear to your actors how much emotional power can be contained in a committed physical gesture like hugging. Most of your students will report that hugging their prop with commitment produced a spontaneous and strong emotion. If your class is mature enough to handle it, have them try some person-to-person hugging as well. It will quickly tune them in to the power of a fully committed physical action onstage. Remind them how in their acting, they often act a hug rather than actually do it, act reading a book rather than really read it, or act looking for something rather than really looking. This is an important message to get across.

ROUND 2
In this round, ask your students to pound their pillows or stuffed animals with their fists. Urge them to pound with commitment. Make sure each of your students is at a safe distance from the others so only the pillows are the recipients of their fists of fury. It may be a good idea to have your students on their knees with their props on the floor to insure accuracy and strength of delivery. As your students are pounding, you may want to coach them by telling them to really hate their pillows, really want to hurt their pillows badly. Again, when you are sure there has been full commitment, end the activity. This time you will no doubt find that the guys have less trouble committing to the exercise. When the room has settled down and heart rates are near normal, have your students discuss what they observed during the activity and what conclusions might be drawn from their observations.

DISCUSSION
Anger is an emotion that is almost always connected with some kind of physical action. The very nature of anger demands a physical outlet. Trying to conjure anger in the abstract, or any other emotion, for that matter, is infinitely harder for most actors than finding the action that conjures up that emotion. Besides, abstract emotion does not forward the story, but an action that carries the emotion will propel the script forward and make the work clear and exciting for the audience. You may want to direct the discussion to other physical actions that clearly, specifically,

and dramatically communicate anger in a storytelling context. You may also want to try some. It will make for an exciting and informative class.

Round 3

This time ask your students to caress their pillows or stuffed animals. You'll probably need to give your class a pep talk beforehand. Loaded words like *caress* can spell danger to the less mature actors in your class; for them, their desire to avoid committing to the activity will be strong. It becomes your responsibility to determine, before beginning, who is onboard and to have those who cannot make the commitment sit the exercise out. Otherwise, the uncommitted actors will disrupt the exercise and prevent the others from getting maximum benefit from the activity.

After the exercise begins, you may want to side coach by encouraging your students to imagine someone they love and pretend that the prop is that person. Remind your students that the imaginary person need not be a lover if that is too much for them to handle, but any loved one, such as a parent, a sibling, or a friend. Who they choose to receive the caress will affect the manner and location of the caress. Caressing the cheek of a daughter may be different than caressing the cheek of a girlfriend. Different actions might be associated with different body parts. Caressing an arm may be executed differently than caressing a neck.

Suggest to your students that if they imagine a specific situation as well as a specific reason for the caress, their work is liable to be more connected and full. Also suggest that they arbitrarily change the manner in which they are stroking and observe what differences result, if any. Keep reminding your students to make mental notes about what they are thinking and feeling.

Discussion

This round reintroduces the concept of choice and specificity. In the earlier rounds, your students should have discovered the power of committing physically to an action. Now, rather than simply coming up with and committing to that action, they are being asked to select a way of executing that action so that it tells much more specifically what a character is thinking and feeling. It should also tell an audience something specific about the nature of the relationship between the character and his prop. Too often actors, especially beginning actors, rely on the first choice that comes to mind or body, and if they are given no negative feedback on this perfunctory choice, that choice remains throughout the rehearsal process. This round should make your students realize they can so specifically define and refine their actions that they become artistic contributions to the work. Most choices are not the result of divine inspiration, but rather a magical collaboration between craft and spontaneous in-the-moment emotional interplay.

ROUND 4

In this round ask your students to return to the caress of the previous exercise. Only this time, before beginning, ask them to imagine a specific set of circumstances for the activity—who they are, who the pillow is, the location of the activity, the time, and so on. As the exercise unfolds, keep reminding your students to be specific, not only in the manner of caressing, but also in the location that is touched. As mentioned in the last round, a caress takes on a different quality depending on the relationship between the characters and when and where the action happens. When your students have finished the activity, ask them to completely change the given circumstances they are working with. Continue to have your students change their given circumstances. This exercise can be repeated with the hugging and the punching actions as well.

DISCUSSION

After several changes in the given circumstances, stop the activity and, as in previous rounds, discuss the observations and draw conclusions about what your students experienced. This round is a further refinement of the work begun in Round 3. Because you set up the parameters beforehand, your students must think about a lot of things before they can determine how they will carry out their assigned physical action. Each of the W's in the given circumstances can and should have a profound influence on the choices they make: Is it a caress in the dark or light, in the bedroom or the public library, by fifteen-year-olds or fifty-year-olds? The more specific your actors can make their choices, the more telling the executed choices will be for them and for the audience. It is important for you to make your students understand that by narrowing down the categories available to them, it will be easier for them to recognize or discover that best possible choice, whether planned or spontaneous.

ROUND 5

For this round, ask your students to repeat the first three rounds (hugging, punching, and caressing, without and then with the given circumstances) with one additional requirement: This time while engaging in each activity, have your students recite a nursery rhyme as if they were saying the rhyme to the pillow or stuffed animal. Instruct your students not to worry about the recitation or the words per se; instead they should focus on their action and their reason for engaging in the action. When all the actions have been completed, you should once again direct a discussion, focusing on the interconnection of words and action during the exercises.

DISCUSSION

The addition of dialogue in this round points up a very important concept. Plays and scenes are not about dialogue, they are about the story being told. Dialogue is a tool for telling the story and is no more or less important than other storytelling tools the playwright may use at any particular time. Hugging, pounding, and caressing are all strong actions, and when a character onstage is doing any one of those activities, chances are the dialogue falls behind those actions in storytelling power and focus. Your student actors should find that their nursery rhymes are shaped more by the physical action being executed than by the content of the words themselves because the dialogue is less dramatically important in the context of the story than the action. On the other hand, they will probably also discover that saying dialogue while committing to an action directed at an object (or person) gives the words a power and an immediacy in accordance with the action being executed and the need being pursued. This need will come out through the dialogue more strongly, more specifically, and more spontaneously than when the words are considered separate from the action taking place. The nursery rhyme will be enriched by the context of the scene as well as the subtext that the given circumstances have provided. This is an enormously important concept essential for understanding how a scene works when reading it and for making the choices that will bring the scene to life on the stage.

Wrap-up

These exercises are not meant to suggest that any time your students want to make a strong moment or scene they should run for the pillow. The objects your actors eventually choose for a scene must be organic to the work they are developing and to the script. But there can be no doubt that using props with commitment and in a well-thought-out fashion can complement, add to, and reveal the story, as well as reveal important character information.

In Hug a Pillow, Slug a Pillow, the prop pillow served as a substitute for other things. But even though the hugging, caressing, and punching was not about the stuffed animals or pillows per se, the specificity your students brought to their props helped make their acting both clear and exciting.

Props and Common Senses

This exercise and the one following, Character Business, employ the concepts introduced in the pillow rounds but require your students to use their props directly. When using their props in these exercises, your actors will need the same degree of commitment and specificity that they gave to their pillows. In addition their selected actions will need to both communicate who they are and tell their stories.

Purpose

Business, any ongoing activity that actors engage in during the course of a scene, often entails the use of a prop. Creating believable business onstage can be more difficult than it appears, especially for today's "from the neck up" actors. But, in spite of the difficulty your students may have with business during scene work, its mastery can make their work onstage more believable and compelling. The purpose of this exercise, then, is to get your students to tell a compelling story while using a prop. The exercise requires your students to communicate a sensory perception to the audience only through physical actions.

Method

Have your students select a piece of business from the list below, and then create a one-minute exercise in which they tell a story that involves one or more of their senses.

- drinking liquor
- drinking a soft drink
- eating a particular food
- eating a meal
- smelling something foul
- smelling something pleasant

- touching something that is sore

- touching something that feels good

- looking through a telescope, microscope, binoculars

- listening to something through headphones, through a wall

After students get feedback from the class, have them repeat the exercise, using the class's criticism and suggestions. For their second rendition, they should be more specific about the details of their choices. Have the class compose a list of detailed questions that each actor can use to make his exercise as specific as possible.

DISCUSSION

Your students will be amazed at how attention to detail in planning and execution will improve and deepen what they do and what they feel. The more detail that actors provide themselves with, the more specific and clear the results. Is the apple they choose to eat mushy or hard, sweet or sour, big or small? How do they feel about apples? Do they like them, hate them, or love them? Are they hungry, or not? Your students should find that this attention to detail stimulates real feeling in them, and their truthful behavior should result in exciting pieces of work.

Character Business

Purpose

This last exercise is one that will allow your students to apply what they have learned about props and business to an actual character from a play they have been studying. The choices they make for this exercise need to be connected with what they know about the character based on their reading and must be supported or implied by the script. The unspoken scene should somehow illuminate the character being portrayed while being consistent with the story as written.

Method

Ask your students to create a one-minute silent scene based on a character and prop from the list below or from other suggestions you may offer. The story your students create should be consistent with the given circumstances of the play, the scene, and the character. Make sure your students have carefully read the play they select and have paid particular attention to the scene that has inspired this new addition. Your students should write up a detailed score that breaks down all the physical actions they will execute during the exercise in chronological order. This will help them build a scene that has a beginning, middle, and end. It will also ensure that the story being told is clear and interesting. The scene should be well rehearsed before it is presented in class.

The Crucible	Elizabeth, a poppet
	Abigail, a poppet
Death of a Salesman	Willy, a rubber hose
	Kate, a rubber hose
	Biff, a rubber hose
The Glass Menagerie	Laura, a glass animal
Macbeth	Macbeth, a dagger
	Lady Macbeth, a dagger
Othello	Othello, a handkerchief
	Desdemona, a handkerchief
	Iago, a handkerchief
Romeo and Juliet	Juliet, a vial of poison
	Romeo, a vial of poison or sleeping potion

A Streetcar Named Desire	Blanche, a tiara
A Zoo Story	Jerry, a knife
	Peter, a knife

DISCUSSION

After each presentation, the class should discuss all aspects of the performance. Was it believable, interesting? Did it make clear some new elements of character or specifically bring out traits that were already known but not previously seen in the play as written? What new elements of character were demonstrated? How was this accomplished? What things were not clear or could be improved? Ask for suggestions for improvement.

Wrap-up

If the actions your students selected and executed were consistent with the characters they were playing, those actions probably helped make the overall story clearer and revealed new aspects about their chosen characters as well. Further, the use of props probably helped connect your students with one or more of their primary senses in a way that imagination alone probably would not.

Hopefully, this sequence of exercises made your students more aware that props can stimulate emotion as well as the senses. In turn, this stimulation will often result in exciting and believable acting choices that are both specific and unexpected—results guaranteed to generate interesting actors telling interesting stories that well serve and enhance the play. This, of course, is the primary obligation of all good actors.

Using Categories: Analysis Through Relationship and Location

During my grad school and professional acting days, my father would regularly tick me off by praising my ability to memorize lines. Back stage after many a show, he would approach me and say something like, "You were amazing. How did you manage to learn all those lines?" He might have said, "You were wonderful. I hardly recognized you as your character. You were so different than you are in life!" Or, "You brought me to tears with the way you played your death scene." Or even, "What a riveting performance!" The truth is he may have thought all those things, but obviously what struck him most was the memorization.

Why did all the other aspects of my performances, the aspects that I held in far greater esteem, take second place for my father and, no doubt, for many other civilians? The tough emotional displays that actors do onstage at a climactic moment will grab audience members' attention and impress them. But most of the believable interaction and choice-making that actors do goes on unnoticed or underappreciated because the acting process, when well done, often looks easy. Actors do onstage what all of us, as social creatures, do most of the day: We act. Social acting is not all that different from onstage or on-screen acting, except actors make and then carry out their acting choices specifically—which, ironically, is at the very heart of fine acting.

Human beings spend a good part of their lives acting out social roles. We are continuously put into social positions in which we are expected to behave in a certain manner, and for the most part, because we are trained to recognize these specific social requirements, we do so with efficiency and economy. None of us, for example, is quite the same at the workplace as we are at home. We show different sides of ourselves in different circumstances. We all play the roles of parent, child, friend, employee, boss, teacher, or student, depending on what is expected of us at a particular time, and we make further adjustments in accordance with where we are when we play those particular roles. We have plenty of reason to do so, since the proper kind of behavior usually gets us what we want, or, at least, keeps us from outcomes we don't want.

Categorizing the roles and tactics people automatically employ to survive and succeed socially can help student actors to narrow down the infinite number of acting choices available to them. With practice your actors can develop their ability to define their setting and relationships in a particular acting situation and from that analysis begin to distill and refine their acting choices. By doing so they can turn a daunting number of possibilities into a more manageable number.

Here, then, is a sequence of exercises that can help your students think in terms of categories. Obviously, fine actors do more than simply categorize situations when deciding how to play a scene, but starting the choice selection process with common sense and logic can be of enormous help, especially for those learning their craft. Once your students have begun to explore the concept, they should be better able to find and make interesting and useful choices when they next approach their scripted work.

Difficult Relationships

Purpose
This exercise is intended to help your students develop the ability to recognize and employ the inherent dramatic possibilities of an acting situation by using relationship categories to narrow down the available circumstances.

Method
ROUND 1
You can begin this improvisational exercise by having your students brainstorm with you. Ask them to suggest dramatic situations that two actors could play out quickly for the class. Write the suggestions on the board, and when a healthy list has been generated, discuss each item for its dramatic possibilities. Once all the suggestions have been discussed, eliminate those items with

the least dramatic potential and begin a series of two-character improvisations, giving as many members of your class as possible a chance to work. You may side coach if absolutely necessary, but try to let your actors find their way to some climax or conclusion on their own. If the first few pairs seem to be wandering in a similar manner, feel free to stop the improvisation and try imposing a one- or two-minute time limit with the remainder of your students. When your list of situations has been used up or all your students have had a chance to work, discuss with your class what you saw and heard.

DISCUSSION
Evaluating each of the suggested situations with your class will allow you to return to the topic of conflict, or engine of drama, and remake the connection between conflict and acting objectives. By determining the potential conflict in each acting situation and by projecting how each of the two roles fits into that conflict, you will create a mechanism for evaluation. It will also reinforce in your students the basic acting concept of finding and playing the best possible story, usually associated with the conflict the playwright creates in his work.

In spite of this discussion, however, it is likely that the improvisations your students put on will be, for the most part, less than dramatically effective—unless your students have had a chance to discuss beforehand the specific given circumstances of each particular scene. For the first round, that should be avoided. A good conflict without a clear idea of the two characters involved is likely to keep the dramatic engine from staying on the track. After some wandering and a lot of random dialogue, a few of the improvs might produce a good pair of whos that, once established, may chug along effectively. Unfortunately, however, it will take so long to establish those specifics that the possibility for creating effective drama will be lost.

ROUND 2

Have your students come up with a list of relationships they can use for the second round. You might start with the good relationship possibilities that they stumbled on in the previous round and then add additional pairs until your class has a significant list to choose from. Your list might include the following:

parent and child

teacher and student

doctor and patient

general and private

coach and player

master and slave

lawyer and client

boss and employee

When your list is finished, repeat the improvisation situations from Round 1 or add new ones. This time assign your students specific relationship roles and see what happens. After the improvs are completed, discuss the results of this round and compare them to the outcomes of the first round.

DISCUSSION

Once your actors have been assigned a role in a relationship, the resulting information will both inform whatever conflict the two are engaged in as well as define specific needs that each of your actors has within that conflict. Suppose, for instance, that the selected conflict is over what show to watch on TV. Without any character clues, your students would be forced to rely on themselves as performers only. They would be tempted to go for the joke, or step outside the scene and comment on it for a laugh or to avoid any discomfort from not knowing what to do. But as soon as they are assigned a relationship tag, that all changes. How would a mother and daughter engage in this particular conflict? Or a father and son? Father and daughter? Simply go down the list and you will see that the relationship clues in each pairing go a long way toward making the conflict over what to watch on TV more specific and filled with believable possibilities to play out.

The resulting scenes should be far better than the ones played out the first time through. The relationship clues, in all likelihood, will have provided the necessary bread crumbs for your acting pairs to find their way through the dramatic forest. Feel free to mix and match the relationship list your students have accumulated with their list of dramatic situations. The possibilities are almost endless. After each improvisation is completed, be sure to discuss what works and why.

Remember, the purpose here is to get your actors to define the conflict and turn it into the best possible story, believably executed. Treat the improvs like drills that a basketball coach might use. The idea is to get the team to respond to the dramatic cues automatically so that in a real game situation, they don't have to think about what to do when a particular situation arises. Once actors can respond that way, it makes it much easier for them to stay in the moment and be available to respond spontaneously to it.

Two-Line Dramas

Purpose
This exercise is similar but more sophisticated than the previous one. It does, however, share its predecessor's primary objectives: to develop your students' ability to recognize the inherent dramatic possibilities in any acting situation and to develop their ability to use relationship categories, hidden or implied, in any acting situation. The ability to recognize dramatic potential is an essential component to any acting success, and this recognition

is possible even with only two lines of dialogue, as this exercise demonstrates. Further, by getting your actors to narrow down and define the usable relationship circumstances available to them, they can turn the fruits of their analysis into exciting and playable choices.

Method

This time ask your students to brainstorm and then write dialogue couplets (a single line of dialogue for each of two characters). Read the couplets aloud a pair at a time, and have your class discuss the possibilities inherent in each. The discussion should focus on which couplets have the greatest potential as possible two-line dramas. Alternatives to this approach might be for you to provide your class with couplets that you have written in advance and then conduct the discussion as described above. You could also elicit spontaneous suggestions from your class and write their suggestions on the board. When a significant list has been generated, discuss each for its dramatic potential.

Once you have agreed on the most useful couplets, you can use the relationship pairs your class came up with in the previous exercise, or you can continue the brainstorming process to find additional pairs to use for this round. Next have your students determine and discuss the core of each of these relationships. In your discussion, try to lead your students to the connection between relationship and conflict, which will help them make strong and interesting acting choices. It will then be relatively easy to convert those two lines of dialogue into moments of drama that will tell a story onstage.

When your discussion is complete, your students will be ready to rehearse their two-line drama. Divide your class into pairs and give them what you think is an appropriate amount of time to work on their scenes. Each pair can use the same dialogue, or you may want to assign different couplets to different pairs. In either case, each pair should select one relationship from the list to play. This exercise can be done as an in-class activity or as a homework assignment. When your students have completed their rehearsal, either in class or as an assignment, critically watch each scene. After each is presented, discuss each for its believability, clarity, and dramatic effect: Was it as interesting as it could have or should have been? Focus particularly on how each pair established and used the defined relationship as the basis for their scene. If the class doesn't know beforehand what the relationship is, then how well the actors communicate the relationship to the audience becomes an important part of the discussion. After the class review, your students should rework the scene using the input they have received. Repeat the process.

If you have a strong class, you could assign each pair to do more than one relationship, so they will have several two-line scenes to rehearse. The presentations and follow-up discussions with this format should be particularly interesting since each group will have had the experience of using the same lines to produce different kinds of scenes. An essential part of the postgame evaluation is whether the character relationships have been made clear through the acting choices themselves and the effectiveness of their execution.

DISCUSSION

Thinking in terms of relationship is not really a new concept; it is simply a magnification of the who aspect of any list of given circumstances. But thinking in these terms enables students to examine the who element in a way they might not think of doing. You may have asked your students detailed questions and tried hard to provide specific guidance, but likely they often forget most of it once they put that scene on its feet. No matter how good an actor is in moment-to-moment work, the resulting scene often makes little dramatic sense, or the characters are not believable because the seemingly more important dialogue has completely usurped the given circumstances.

It is essential, then, that you keep reminding your actors that scenes are about conflict, and the kind of conflict generated is often connected to the relationship of the characters. Take the following prosaic dialogue couplet, for example:

A: Where have you been?
B: I went for a walk.

If this dialogue couplet is suggested by someone in your class, the discussion might result in the following conclusions. The question asked by A seems adversarial, and the response by B seems terse and could indicate an unwillingness by B to provide more detail than absolutely necessary. Why has the question been asked and why is there such a dearth of information in the response? Since there are no other facts to draw from, the relationship between these characters will be very important.

Now let's assign the teacher/student relationship tag to this couplet. Knowing that the exchange is between a teacher and student raises more questions. Under what circumstances would a student disappear from the classroom? Does the scene occur before or after school, or during the class itself? Did the student walk out of a detention? Was the teacher angry, worried, shocked, or simply curious? All of these? None of these?

Note the jump to clarity once we define the relationship, whether as teacher/student, parent/child, or husband/wife. The simple tag of relationship goes a long way toward providing background information that can help determine how to say the lines. A relationship tag also provides insight about how each actor may react to the spoken lines. The relationship tag automatically forces your actors to deal with a host of given circumstances, so easy to ignore when the tag is not assigned. By assigning a relationship, we open the door to excellent possibilities that would have otherwise remained undiscovered.

Let's examine the dialogue under the umbrella of husband and wife. When we look at the dialogue pair with this relationship in mind, the opening question might be asked by either the husband or the wife. Will your class realize that, or will they make the traditional assumption that it is the wife who asks the opening question? Sometimes actors are too quick to draw conclusions, and they miss interesting dramatic possibilities. If the husband asks the question, rather than the wife, how does that change things? Why? An interesting discussion is possible here. Is the fact that the opening question is delivered without any terms of endearment significant? Does the husband/wife relationship tag color the "I went for a walk" line differently than it did in the teacher/student relationship? Why or why not? The answer is probably yes. In the previous relationship, the answer seems like a legitimate factual response. In this situation, the response could be an avoidance device or an outright lie.

Either of these possibilities would lead to a set of good dramatic choices for the scene. By raising these questions, it quickly becomes apparent that other given circumstances need to be addressed. Time and location in particular could strongly affect how this couplet is played by your actors, and many variations on the scene are possible—each of them offering wonderful dramatic potential.

The analogy for scene work that these exercises suggest becomes obvious. As mentioned earlier, students love to throw out the homework they have done on a scene once they put the scene on its feet. They return to the literal meaning of the dialogue and forget the context and subtext that the given circumstances provide, which should be shaping the unfolding story. Imposing a relationship between characters in a scene is like tying a string around an actor's finger: When he thinks of relationship, he will almost automatically resurrect the rest of the who, what, when, and where, which will usually put a scene on the right track.

CATEGORIZING LOCATION

The social acting we learn to do is not dependent only on the particular relationship roles we play. The kinds of social acting choices we make are also dependent on where we are playing these particular roles as well as any number of other things. But where a particular event happens to play out in life often affects the manner in which it is played out. Here is an example. Suppose the following dialogue couplet is used to play out a scene between two people who have been seeing each other.

A: I love you.

B: I love you too.

Obviously, who they are and their particular relationship is extremely important in making the choices that will make this scene work, but let's skip over that for a moment. Instead, let's focus only on where the scene takes place. Suppose, for instance, that it takes place in the bleachers while a big football game is in progress. How does that affect the dialogue delivery? Now suppose it takes place in A's office while coworkers conduct their business around A and B. How does this scenario affect line delivery? Now suppose it takes place in a cozy, romantic restaurant, or alone in a car: same question. Now that you've thought through the answers, you may want to try this exercise with your class. But even if you don't, it is obvious that each of these locale adjustments will make for different kinds of acting choices.

The goal of the exercise is to have your students identify or choose the specific setting for a scene and to convert that choice into appropriate acting choices. All too often, however, they will have trouble selecting a location. So, as with the relationship categories, you can help your students narrow down the choices available by organizing locations into helpful categories. Years ago, a good acting teacher of mine suggested the following categories, and they have since worked for me:

In *public space*, people have almost unrestricted access. They can come and go as they like and can freely observe each other. As an exercise, your class might want to make a list of such locations.

In *private space*, access is much more restricted, but the space is still shared and those allowed access are free to come and go. Your class might want to compose a list of private space as well.

In *personal space*, an individual has total control, and the coming and going of others can be restricted by its owner. Again, your students might compose a list of these locales.

Feel free to adopt or adapt these categories for your class. The important point here is to give your students a way to recognize a location and narrow down their choices to selections that will work for them. People behave differently in different locations. It is the actor's job to create the kind of behavior that will be appropriate for the selected location.

Once your students have a grasp on their location categories, you can try some simple improvs using location and situation. Later, you can go back to the previous exercises on relationship and let your students discover how these combined categorizations can help them in their work.

Wrap-up

When done well, acting looks easy because, as human beings, we all act every day. We modify our behavior in accordance with where we are and with whom. Most of us adapt to our environment and to the relationships in which we are engaged, often without thinking about it. But as actors, a little thought can spell the difference between a good choice and a bad one, between one that serves the story being told and one that does not. Thinking about the relationship between characters and location can provide students with vital clues to making choices that really work well. As these exercises demonstrate, relationship and location can strongly and positively affect how students play out their selected actions.

Language and Style

When Hurricane Floyd threatend Florida, I overheard two freshman acting students who were not from Miami discussing the hurricane's imminent arrival. In Miami, it was quickly becoming an almost panic situation, and to these two non-natives, the atmosphere was clearly growing very scary. The pair were talking about death and devastation, and their eyes and body language clearly reflected their fear. Yet, if I had been listening to their dialogue without watching them, I frankly would have become bored almost instantly. Their phrasing was flat; they used upspeak; their choice of words was cliché-ridden; and they interrupted any potential dramatic progression in their phrasing with an infinite number of place-holding "likes" as in, "It's, like, getting, like, really scary around here."

If the language use I've described sounds familiar to you, then you probably face a dilemma familiar to many acting teachers—trying to make young actors grasp one of their most, if not *the* most, important tool—language. We have heard over and over in recent years that today's generation is more visual than aural and oral. They have grown up on movies and computer games, not on books, theater, and radio. Even their music is built as much on visuals, provided by MTV videos, as it is on music and lyrics. In a way, we should be grateful for rap music, even if we hate it, since its core depends on a lot of words that must be listened to carefully.

We can rationalize or lament our students' inability to use language well in their everyday life, but how do we address this insensitivity in their acting work? In general, today's students are oblivious to the specific meaning, power, nuance, subtext, and poetry of words as they are used individually and together by the dramatic wordsmith—the playwright.

Clearly, for theater acting this is an untenable situation. Plays, modern or classical, clearly rely primarily on the dialogue the playwright has used. This dialogue, even when sounding like ordinary speech has been specifically selected and shaped by its author to produce an effect. Flat reading by actors in a work by Shakespeare will quickly drive an audience toward the exit signs. But even in contemporary writing, a student's inability to color a phrase, or her insistence on using upspeak at a particular dramatic moment, can destroy the tension.

So, what do we do? In previous chapters, I discussed the importance of using words effectively and of the insensitivity so many young actors today have toward a playwright's words. I offered several ways to get students to begin using their words more effectively. In this chapter I offer another sequence of exercises that, I hope, will bring your actors along that trail.

Announcer Training

In the old days, standard procedure for training language insensitivity in actors might include reciting poetry aloud—an Emily Dickinson or Robert Frost poem, for instance. For the less verbally challenged, perhaps a Shakespeare sonnet, or even a short soliloquy by the bard, could be analyzed for its mechanics and figurative language. This approach, no doubt, still works today if your students truly have the skills to take it on. If your students are like many of mine, however, you might want to first try the following.

Method

Have your students find a newspaper or magazine ad for a product or service; an ad that lasts about thirty seconds when read will do fine. Assign them to read their ads to the class one at a time. Solicit feedback from the class after each reading. Discuss whether the ad has been effectively rendered. Does the reading effectively sell the product or service described in the ad? If the class thinks the reading was effective, which specific elements did the reader use to make it so? Which elements needed to be improved? If the ad was not effectively rendered, what was lacking in the reading, and why?

DISCUSSION

The first thing your class should consider is that the purpose of any ad is to sell a product or service. Selling necessitates convincing the audience to buy. In acting terms, this is identical to playing an intention or objective. The words in the ad should, therefore, be inflected, shaped, and arranged to sell that product or service. The task here is not unlike that of the trial lawyer in his summation speech. Which pieces of information will most help the defendant? The lawyer must put these pieces together in such a way that the jury has no choice but to agree with his argument. With an ad, it becomes the actor's responsibility to find the most sellable points and emphasize them in the reading. Examine the following copy.

> Your eyes must be lying. That's what you'll be thinking the first time you view Apex High Definition TV. A picture so vivid it can't be a picture. Apex High Definition TV—it doesn't get any more real than this.

The first question is, of course, which words help sell the product the most? Those words must be emphasized if the ad is to be read effectively. The second question is how can you turn the copy into an interesting throughline? As with all well-acted material, the actor must find a logical dramatic progression in the delivery to keep the material interesting to the audience. Once your students can isolate the words that sell, deliver them effectively, and put the whole piece together in a dramatically interesting way, they are beginning to get language sensitive. You might want to try a longer, more sophisticated ad, or move on.

The Children's Book

Last winter I had the privilege of seeing *Wit,* the multi-award-winning Off-Broadway play, while I was recruiting in New York. At the climax of the play, one of the characters reads *The Runaway Bunny* by Margaret Wise Brown. That reading was one of the most moving and memorable theatrical moments I have ever witnessed. The simple poetry and wisdom contained in the words of this children's classic, a book that I have read countless times to my own daughter, came alive during that reading in a way it had never done before. In part it was the context in which the reading in the play occurred, but it was also because the actor reading the book made maximum use of what was available to her—the individual words and their arrangement.

Method

Ask your students to prepare an oral reading of a short illustrated children's book for class. Margaret Wise Brown, Maurice Sendak, Eric Carle, P. D. Eastman, and, of course, Dr. Seuss are all effective sources for this exercise. The reading should not be an excerpt. These illustrated children's books were meant to be read aloud in their entirety, and that's just what your students should do.

After each presenter has completed his reading, your students should evaluate what they heard. Discuss whether the reading was effectively rendered.

Did the reader use key words actively and colorfully? If it was so, how did the reader make them colorful?

Did the verbs contain action? Were the adjectives specific?

If word usage was colorless, what was lacking? If it was sometimes colorful and sometimes not, analyze the difference.

Were the repetitions in the story dramatically interesting?

Was each repetition different from the previous one? How was each different?

Was the difference dramatically effective?

Did each repetition help propel the story forward?

Did the story build effectively toward its climax? Why or why not?

Did the reader make good use of humor? If so, how was this accomplished?

If not, why? How could the reader have made better use of humor?

Did the reader stimulate vivid mental pictures in the listeners?

Did the word pictures live up to or surpass the book illustrations?

Did the reading make the good things sound good and the bad things sound bad?

Were the good and bad things referred to specific or generalized? Why?

Did the narrator have a personality or an attitude about the material, about the characters in the story, about the listeners?

All these things must be considered by the reader, for they are all part of the storyteller's responsibility. Besides, in a children's story, all these issues are, at the least, suggested by the words themselves and by their arrangement.

DISCUSSION

In many picture books for children, the author uses a formula that is established, built on, and repeated. Even small children pick up on this formula very quickly, as they are intended to, which creates joyful expectation. As the formula is maintained and built on, the story progresses, moving toward an exciting climax. The excitement comes from the danger and difficulty the escalating formula presents to the reader as well as from the music that the word patterns themselves create. The escalating verbal excitement is like the excitement experienced when kids build a skyscraper with blocks; each additional piece placed on the one below literally heightens the tension and suspense.

This formula is used to excellent effect by Dr. Seuss in several of his most popular beginners' reading books, such as *Green Eggs and Ham* or in both of his Cat in the Hat books. The list of "do not like them's" in the former and the lists of number and letter characters in the latter make excellent wordplay combinations of comedy and drama. They also provide actors with a playground for developing their abilities in building dramatic tension vocally and coloring long lists of nouns and adjectives with specifics that might otherwise become generalized and ineffectual. The picture books that have survived for generations make the most effective use of words. It is the actor's job to develop what's provided on the printed page and make it specific. When your students' vocal coloring and dynamics do justice to the words on the printed page, then you might want to try the following exercise.

Pledge of Allegiance

Most of us learned the Pledge of Allegiance in kindergarten or thereabouts. Most, if not all the concepts contained therein, were probably beyond us at the time, and for many of us, by the time we were old enough to consider what it was we were actually saying, we were already saying the entire thing by rote. For that reason, the Pledge of Allegiance makes an excellent script for the next word sensitivity exercise.

The pledge provides several useful challenges for the student reciting it. First, its construction is formal. Most of us would seldom use phrases like "I pledge allegiance" or "for which it stands." Second, the pledge also contains several concept words that should conjure up strong connotative pictures and feelings in the speaker. Liberty and justice would, for most people, be filled with meaning when used in the appropriate context. Phrases such as "one nation" and "under God" should be filled with feeling as well. That is not the case, however, with the pledge, since most of us never think about the words when we have occasion to say them at formal gatherings—usually at school functions where we are expected to both pledge our allegiance and sing the national anthem. Most of us are too busy checking each other out to focus on what we are singing and saying. On the rare occasions when we are called upon to make our oaths, in times of national crisis or tragedy, for instance, the words suddenly come into focus and possess a resonance that at most other times simply does not exist. That is what gave me the idea for this exercise.

Method
ROUND 1
After reciting the Pledge of Allegiance as a group (to get rid of cobwebs and tongue-ties), ask your students to come in front of the class one at a time and recite the pledge individually. Make no instructive comments; simply remind your class that this is

an acting exercise. Allow each member to perform his version of the pledge.

DISCUSSION
In this first round, you put your students in a difficult acting scenario. Because you introduced no given circumstance to focus their thinking as actors, many will flounder when left to their own devices. They will not think about what you are asking them to do and, as a result, will probably come up with little that is dramatically effective and merely recite the words. Your more savvy students, even if they don't come up with a specific context to play out, will use the other acting tools available to them and, since there are no given circumstances, will likely focus on the words themselves.

In your follow-up discussion, emphasize that you reminded them at the beginning of the exercise that this was about acting, not reciting. They should never forget that good acting always entails believability in combination with telling the best possible story and serving the script. If they simply recited, they left out the acting headwork essential in any acting situation.

Begin the discussion by soliciting comments from your students about the recitations. If your class needs a prompt, you might start with these questions:

Which one or ones do you remember best? Why?

What about each of them was memorable, effective, or noteworthy? Why?

With guidance, your class will soon be talking of dramatic throughline, commitment, high stakes, specificity, and use of language.

In all likelihood, the pieces singled out as more memorable will be those in which the actors colored the words with specificity and spoke with some sense of personalization. In other noteworthy ones, students took on personas other than their own. If that is the case, your discussion should focus on whether the character choice and the script recited were connected and whether those two elements worked together to produce a coherent and meaningful dramatic throughline. Did the script and characterization work together to make a clear and interesting story? Or was the reading overacted, masking actor discomfort at having to go to the front of the room and recite? It is important to instill in your students that the purpose of any choices they make should be to serve and contribute to the story being created or interpreted. Their purpose should never be to show off—to perform in an entertaining fashion or use the script as a distraction from their personal discomfort. Once they can make choices that are committed to and amplify the words they are saying, they are ready to take on the next round.

ROUND 2

In this round, given circumstances are added—the who, what, when, and where that can double the resonance of the words. Feel free to make up your own situations, but I have found one that is consistently effective: the stakes are high, the scene is climactic, and the group atmosphere is such that your students will probably feed off each other's concentration and commitment. Inform your class that they must improvise a scene in which you are their teacher in the last session of a citizenship-training course. They must all select a country to hale from, decide how old they are, and formulate the background that brought them to this moment. They should determine their attitude about this country, their former country, their goals, dreams, and so on. Once they have thought through their given circumstances, they should think about the script (in this case the Pledge of Allegiance) and how the words can be used to suggest their created background information in the strongest way possible. Obviously, not everything from their fictional background can be used directly while reciting the Pledge of Allegiance, but the pledge should be delivered with that background in mind.

You might want to make the given circumstances a written

homework assignment to be done before you attempt the exercise in class. This will better ensure that your students think carefully about their character, rather than make on-the-spot arbitrary choices that may not be dramatically effective. Be sure to tell your students that the character they develop must translate into acting choices when they do the assignment in class. When it is time to actually begin the exercise in class, role-play your part to the hilt. You might begin with something like:

> Good evening class. It is with great pride that I welcome you to the last class session we have together before your citizenship examination. You have worked long and hard to get to this point, and each and every one of you has made great sacrifices to get where you are today. As I look around the room, it fills me with joy that we have shared this time together. I know that each of you will continue to make a wonderful contribution to your newly chosen homeland, and I am honored to be sharing this time with you. Will you join me now in saying the Pledge of Allegiance one last time before we say good-bye?

You get the idea. The point is to put your students in the frame of mind that an immigrant might have at this particular moment. Then have your class recite together and see what happens. You can end the improvisation immediately after the pledge, you can continue the improv and simply see what happens, or you could do some side coaching to keep the improv going in the right direction. When you decide it is time to end the improvisation, discuss what the class saw and heard. Try to distill from your class what worked best.

DISCUSSION
Obviously, if your class is all pledging at the same time, their commentary and analysis will, for the most part, focus on their own recitation. If the setup is effective, most, if not all your students, will have found at least some moments where the words and feelings link together with specificity for the characters they

are playing. Many acting lightbulbs will probably go off for them. You should get them to articulate as clearly as possible how the spoken words were different for them this time. You might want to discuss how a recited pledge might be different now, even if they recited it as themselves. In all probability, they will have discovered both a deeper meaning and corresponding feelings about all the words they were saying, and certainly the concept words will now carry far more amplitude than they did before.

LATER ROUNDS

As a follow-up to the exercise described above, I usually do a close-up round next. I ask each student to act the pledge again, one at a time, as if they were doing the movie close-up of the previous group scene. How much of what they did as part of an ensemble can they retain when asked to repeat their work individually? If they were able to articulate what they did in the group ensemble, then at least part of what they did in the earlier exercise should now be tangible and somewhat repeatable. The results are often surprisingly effective.

If you find this exercise has been effective, you can continue along the same lines with these scenarios:

a group of reuniting World War II vets

a group of Vietnam vets

a Boy or Girl Scout troop

a group of first graders

member of an antigovernment militant group

members of the KKK

a disenfranchised minority group

a white supremacy group

Wrap-up

If your students come up with specific background choices as they did with the citizenship class, the results should be interesting and compelling and the words used should create pictures for the audience that are both specific and filled. By the time you have finished the group of exercises described above, your students' words should be conjuring, even if not quite a thousand pictures, then certainly pictures with a lot more colors than they had been previously using. Hopefully, they will have also absorbed how important to any dramatic situation the effective use of a playwright's words can be.

When I Went to the Store, I Bought

One day in class I listened to a beautifully performed monologue by one of my students. This particular monologue did not come from a monologue book, nor did it come from one of those collections containing those oft-repeated original pieces to be used for auditions. The material I heard struck me as fresh and dramatically rich, not so much because of the words themselves but rather because of the singular connection between the words and the actor who spoke them. Part of the monologue went something like this:

> When my father died, he left me his abacus, its beads faded by time and use. He left me his Bible, earmarked to his favorite verses. He also left me his Cadillac DeVille convertible from 1960. When my father died, he left me his dentures still in his glass by the sink, and he left me the elephant head he won for me at a poker game at the county fair. When my father died, he left me a face in the mirror that was his as well as mine, and he left me the ghost that stands behind that reflected face. When my father died, he left me heartbroken and helplessly alone.

As she mentioned each item, the memory of it washed over her, and she seemed to change: each item held a specific meaning for her, and the memories associated with each item returned to her as she spoke the words. For this actor, the words had become almost tangible images, and those images were rich, because they were personal and specific. This, needless to say, illustrates the ideal marriage between actors and the words they use.

That monologue is the product of the following exercise. It was composed improvisationally by a class playing the exercise and refined only slightly by me for reproduction. If you look closely at the monologue, you will find that the items left by the late father of the speaker are arranged in alphabetical order, a mnemonic device to help the actor remember the listed items. Any similarity to the childhood game When I Went to the Store, I Bought is entirely intentional, and that game is the inspiration for the exercise described below.

Purpose

This series of exercises first helps students to better connect the words they use as actors with the objectives they choose to play. Second, it helps young actors deepen the meaning of the words they use for themselves and for the audience that hears them. Words can be powerful tools for the actor, but too often words alone or in combination fail to be fully used by the actors saying them.

Method

ROUND 1

Before beginning the first round of this exercise, remind your students that they are about to begin an acting exercise. Then say something like the following:

> Remember the game "When I Went to the Store" that you
> probably played when you were a kid? That's the game we're

going to play now. The first player will begin with the phrase "When I went to the store, I bought . . ." and come up with an item that begins with the letter A that can be found at the store. The second player will repeat the phrase and item and then add an item that begins with the letter B. Each actor will in turn repeat the phrase and the previous items and add a new item that begins with the next letter of the alphabet. The game continues until a player gets stuck and cannot remember the next item in the list.

Discussion

Your class will immediately forget that this is an acting exercise. Instead they will focus on the memory aspect of the game and play it simply as a contest. All their energies will go into remembering the items; none of their energy will go into making the recitation of the list interesting or meaningful, as an actor would be responsible for doing. When the game finally halts because of memory burnout, remind your class that their focus as actors should have been on communication. Their purpose or objective was to make the listener understand the significance of the words—both in terms of what the item is and what it meant to them.

In real life each item would mean something to a speaker talking about them, and each would have particular physical characteristics: appearance, smell, weight, texture. Which characteristic would have been most significant to the speaker and why? What would have been the attitude of the speaker to that item? The more specific the answer, the more colors available to the actor when he says the word. A quart of milk or a piece of cheese is usually not fraught with dramatic import. But could a container of milk possibly be significant? Could a round of cheese be terribly important to the speaker? Of course they could. The actor must use a personal set of given circumstances to ensure that an importance is created and maintained. It is an actor's responsibility to make his life onstage as dramatically interesting as possible.

On the other hand, it is also true that if each item on the list has equal dramatic importance, or if the items are mundane but played as earth-shattering, the developing monologue could turn out ridiculous. The selection and accumulation of each item must be considered in a context beyond its alphabetic sequence.

Finally, in an acting situation, this list must be communicated to someone and there must be an underlying reason for saying it. Suggest to your actors that it is their responsibility for finding an intention or objective for communicating the list to a listener, and the more specific and stronger the reason, the more dramatically effective the reading will be. Remind your actors that the reason should be somehow connected to the listener. What does the speaker want or need from the listener that justifies his communicating the shopping list to her? Obviously, the higher your actors make the stakes, the more likely they are to make the reading effective.

Round 2

Reinforce for your students that in this round they are not to focus on or worry so much about remembering all the items. Your class can even provide the speaker with the next item if the speaking actor indicates the need for help.

Side coaching is fine since the focus should now be shifted toward using the words rather than remembering them. Coach your students into visualizing each item, using all their available senses before they actually say the word. Tell them that this kind of preparation time will allow their imaginative processes to work. If they involve more senses in their preparation, each item will be easier to remember and spoken with more specificity and meaning.

Ask your students to come up with a gesture for each new item that somehow encapsulates physically what that item means to them. The gesture can be broad or realistic, but it should not be arbitrary. If, for instance, the item is brussels sprouts, the gesture might be fingers to nose indicating an unpleasant smell. If the item is a can of cleanser, a rubbing motion might accompany the saying of the word. As a result, the exercise will include both a list of word items shopped for and a series of physical actions that play in sequence and parallel the actual delivery of the words. The game is over when the speaker, even with help, either can no longer remember the next item, or the list becomes so long and unwieldy that it simply makes sense to halt the game. Discuss with your class what they observed in each other's work. Then discuss what they learned about acting in general and about their own work.

DISCUSSION

After the experience of the first round, you will probably notice a marked improvement in your students' ability to focus on and use words and images. There will probably be colors, levels, a use of subtext, and a clear connection between the speaker and the listening group. The speakers will make an observable effort to make the listeners understand the images as they are seen and felt by the speaker. These communication efforts will make the entire list far more dramatically interesting.

In addition, the use of physical action or gesture for each item on the list will palpably help every speaker. The use of actions will make each item clearer and more real for the actor and, therefore, clearer and more specific for the listeners. A commitment to the action invariably affects an expressed word by making it, as a result of that physical commitment, more colored and more specific, even without thinking about the word. This concept was explored in Hug a Pillow, Slug a Pillow. As a quick example say the word *love*. Now say it while stroking your cheek gently. Which love was more filled? That is the principle behind using gestures. The physical commitment will help your student actors find an assortment of subtextual colors that they might not reach simply by using their brains.

ROUND 3

This round of the exercise then is intended not only to simulate what an actor would need to do in a play but stimulate a recognition of what a good playwright does for the actor in the script.

Therefore, it becomes your actors' responsibility to find a way to make the list they will be creating possess a dramatic progression. To do so, your actors will have to address all the issues they would consider were they working on a monologue from a play. In addition they will have to think as a playwright thinks, by offering up items on the shopping list that help create that playable dramatic progression. There is no room in this round for simply adding an item because it begins with the next letter of the alphabet. Instead, each added item must contribute to the unfolding story. For that reason you may want to allow your students to use adjectives and adjectival phrases that strengthen the dramatic power of the items offered up. Make sure, however, that each new item contributed comes before any descriptive flourishes. An item with description might then go something like this: "When I went to the store, I bought an apple, rock hard and fragrant, and I bought a bag of beets to make borscht for grandpa, and I bought a container to keep the beet soup warm."

DISCUSSION
Before beginning this round, it would be a good idea to lead a discussion about the actor's responsibility to the playwright and to the overall story contained in the words of a play, a scene, or, as in this case, an isolated monologue. A playwright who uses a monologue in a play, for instance, has a specific dramatic reason for putting that monologue into the work. Too often young actors consider a monologue to be an action-stopping excursion away from the central story, written to show specific character and emotion, but not adding directly to the flow of dramatic action of the play. But the good playwright has written that monologue as part of the ongoing action; it is meant to expose new depths and aspects of a character, but never at the expense of the ongoing story.

For the list to work dramatically, your students will need a game plan. To develop a dramatic throughline, they should consider the following topics:

- the given circumstances

- the conflict surrounding this speech

- their objectives for citing this shopping list

- the reaction of the listener or listeners that affect the speaker during the speech

- the throughline or journey made by the speaker during the speech

Note that in the borscht example mentioned above, even with only three letters of the alphabet accounted for, a throughline of possible dramatic progression is already being established.

If your students think creating a dramatic monologue is easy, they are, of course, mistaken. Playwriting is seldom easy, and in a way, you will be asking your students to do just what a playwright does, but each of them will be making her playwriting contribution with only a moment to think. Even though there will be no writing involved, the selection process necessary to make this round work is much like the building process that a playwright would no doubt go through were he creating this particular shopping speech for a play. It is important for your students to understand this from the outset, because if they do, they are likely to produce interesting and usable material.

Given Circumstances
You might ask your students if they can recall a time when they told someone about the items they purchased on a shopping junket. Some of your students probably will be able to do so, the reason being that it was likely a successful or unusual shopping trip—terrific bargains, unusual items, unexpectedly finding just the things they wanted or needed or, even better, things they didn't know they wanted or needed but desired as soon as they saw them. Or, as in the borscht case above, the shopping trip might have had an important, specific purpose.

These are the kinds of circumstances that make for good dramatic writing and, in turn, good, compelling acting. After all, plays are written not about the ordinary but about the extraordinary. A good realistic play, though seeming real, focuses on events, selected and controlled by the playwright, that somehow manage to be life altering. Otherwise, the material will not hold an audience. Your students must consider this obligation of good drama before they offer up their contributions to the shopping list monologue. No matter how good they are as actors, they will probably not be able to keep the stakes high if they have to tell only about the Q-Tips and raisins they purchased. If Q-Tips and raisins are the topics of discussion, they had better be special Q-Tips and raisins.

Conflict
Any situation becomes more interesting when a conflict is involved, and this is especially true of an acting situation. But what kind of conflict could be associated with a shopping list? That's where *Head-First Acting* comes in. If conflicts are internal, then what could be the problem between the speaker and the fact that she went shopping and purchased these items? If the conflicts are external—between the speaker and listener, or between the speaker and a nonpresent party—how could or would that affect the speaker? More important, how could this conflict be integrated into the acting situation? You and your students should consider these questions before playing out this round.

Suppose, for instance, the speaker is an overweight person talking to her support group, or a bulimic speaking to her therapist or a few intimate friends who are dubious about her claimed recent improvements. What if the speaker is poor but has recently gotten some money and gone on a shopping spree? How about a foreigner who has never experienced the shopping choices available to an American? How might this affect the speaker internally or set her off from those who have always unappreciatively lived in this manner? As you can see, the possibilities are endless, and each can have a profound influence on how the eventual list might be delivered.

Objectives

As your students should well know by now, conflict and objective are closely associated: the conflict set up by the playwright leads to the need, intention, objective, or action that the actor chooses to play. In this shopping list situation, what does the speaker want to make the listener do? How, by virtue of sharing the shopping list, does the speaker want to change the listener? What does the speaker want the listener to learn as a result of describing the list of purchases? There is no single specific answer in the abstract. But, if you reexamine the hypothetical situations offered in the given circumstances (the bulimic, for instance), then a reason for making the speech can be ascertained by the actor. This kind of consideration should be an important part of the choice-making process of any actor trying to interpret a script.

Using Reactions of Listeners and the Throughline

How the listeners respond to the speaker will invariably affect the way the next item on the list is presented by the speaker and, in turn, will help create a dramatic throughline—the journey that the speaker makes during the course of the monologue. A dramatic situation becomes effective when the speaker delivering the monologue changes during the course of the speech as a result of the conflict he faces during the journey. The victories, defeats, new information, and discoveries made during the journey, either self-made or created through interaction with the listeners, help alter the speaker and create the dramatic journey necessary to good writing and acting.

If the bulimic is sharing her shopping list with her support group, their reactions, positive or negative, will no doubt affect the way she delivers the items on her list. If the speaker is an obese person who has fallen off the wagon and is sharing the shopping list with her support group, her initial enthusiasm might be sharply curtailed as she faces the disappointment and hostility of her listeners. Or, perhaps, her description of the food items purchased becomes a wish fulfillment for her listeners and inspires the speaker to put cherries and whipped cream on the word pictures she paints. An immigrant's view of an American supermarket might open the jaded eyes and ears of listeners who have long taken for granted the bounty available to them. Suppose the speaker is explaining to her relatives how she made and delivered the borscht that grandpa hasn't had in sixty years? In each the speaker-listener relationship offers up wonderful possibilities for dramatic throughlines.

Whatever your class comes up with for given circumstances, you'll probably want to do this round several times: first compiling the usable shopping list of items; next, adding and modifying the descriptive phrases to go along with the actual list items; and finally to developing a throughline that will make the list dramatically effective. Once the list and its modifying phrases have been compiled and worked on, you may want to assign the group-composed monologue as an individual assignment. If you choose to do so, each student can work on the piece independently, rethinking the given circumstances, objectives, and so on, and working to make the shopping list into a compelling dramatic piece that will stand alone. Have your students bring in their work at the designated time, and see what they come up with.

Variations
Using a shopping list in Round 3 may be too challenging for your particular students. If so, you may want to substitute one of the following options:

When I get out of school, I'm going to . . .

When my father died, he left me . . .

These opening lines are far more provocative than the shopping list and will likely jar the imaginations of your students with less prompting. If, on the other hand, you decide to stick with the shopping list, the above suggestions can be used in additional rounds beyond Round 3 and will take the exercise in new directions. You will probably discover that both these first lines conjure up strong emotion-laden possibilities for your students to play out.

Wrap-up

Whether you ultimately do three or more rounds of this exercise, or pick and choose, you will find that, as a result of doing them, your students will have developed a better appreciation and facility for using the words a playwright provides. Students must learn to examine each word the playwright chooses, as well as that word's relationship to the words that surround it. They must also learn to examine the playwright's words in the dramatic context she has provided if they are going to deliver their dialogue with maximum effectiveness. When I Went to the Store should reinforce the power of a playwright's words the next time your students use scripted material. This recognition of and facility with the playwright's primary tool is, of course, a cornerstone of a good actor's art and craft.

Using the Script

Have you ever had the following experience? You're watching a student rehearsing a monologue. The words seem disjointed and she struggles to make sense of the monologue, trying desperately to connect one moment to the next as she searches for that hidden throughline apparently known only by the playwright. Then, as you begin to coach that student, you discover that the iffy piece she's rehearsing is actually the work of a first-rate writer. The student had cut up the piece to make it fit into a time limit or had pruned it, thinking she was improving it. When the missing lines of the monologue, like those jigsaw puzzle pieces lost under the rug, are restored, the monologue suddenly ticks like a Swiss watch—and your actor starts to connect with it as if she had been injected with a week's worth of emotional recall.

The craft and discipline of the skilled playwright is all too often completely taken for granted by those who owe him the most—the actors themselves. Many student actors, and many trained ones, for that matter, underappreciate or ignore outright the treasure map that a first-class playwright creates. Playwrights, like most artists, carefully select and control their material, rewriting until they are sure that the action they have created is clear, economical, and exciting and that the characters they have crafted reveal themselves succinctly through action and word. The well-planned interconnectedness of plot and character is truly a thing of beauty.

The craft of the scriptwriter can easily be appreciated by watching great old films. Whenever I see the really good ones, I am always struck by a number of things seldom credited to the writer. The first is that scenes my memory says took up a lot of screen time turn out to be surprisingly brief. Yet, no matter how fleeting they are, they provide enough information and detail to make the overall story work. Another is that characters, immortally etched into my memory, are often merely suggested rather than fully developed. But, magically, the material works anyway, in spite of its dated hokeyness and, in some cases, bad acting.

Take *Casablanca,* for instance. In my memory, the film details the weeks or months Rick and Ilsa spend together in Paris before the German occupation interrupts their love affair. We learn how their love germinates and blossoms into undying passion. In reality, their time together in Paris has been clocked at about eight minutes of screen time. How then can the audience possibly accept their undying love for each other when it all happens so quickly? Why are we so moved by their tragic sacrifices and their unselfish courage later in the movie based on so little time together on screen? Certainly, Bogart and Bergman deserve credit for their special chemistry on film, but of equal importance is good scriptwriting craft. The best screenwriters, like successful writers for the stage, know how to craft material to make it work.

Everything in a good script is there for a reason, and it is up to the actors to figure it all out and use it. Once they do, like Bogie and Bergman, they can simply swim with the flow of the script. Actors have the responsibility to break that script down into its working parts, so they can serve it effectively. This is brain work, and too often it is neglected When it is, the task of making compelling, exciting theater is made more difficult.

Monologue Makers

Purpose

Monologue Makers is a series of sequential exercises intended to help student actors become more sensitive to the playwright's craft. It will also help them develop the tools to better serve any script. The exercises are designed to:

- give the student actor the opportunity to analyze an event for its story potential

- give the student actor the opportunity to dramatically shape and rearrange a true event

- develop in the actor appreciation for the playwright's craft; how he selects and controls his material and includes only what is needed to tell a story clearly and effectively

- develop in the actor appreciation for the social commentary that good playwrights provide

- give the student actor a chance to bring to dramatic life what she or another student has created by paying attention to what is in the script

Though valuable to do at any time, Monologue Makers is especially effective at the beginning of a semester because it gently leads students into a performance situation. Participating students have a chance to test the performance waters before having to swim outright. Further, they are gently exposed to the fact that good drama enlightens as well as entertains.

Method

ROUND 1

In the first phase of Monologue Makers, all students in the class are asked to relate a true story in which they were either the central character or indirectly related. Many students will be nervous at first. It is always scary to speak to a large group even if the talking is informal. I make my students tell their story in front of the class rather than from their seats. Though this makes the storytelling seem more like a performance, for the shy and self-conscious, it is still less painful than being thrown into a real acting assignment right away.

You might want to be the first storyteller in your class. This will clearly demonstrate that you're a good sport, and your work will also serve as a model for what is expected of them when it's their turn. Suggest to your students that they take notes. You may also want to tell your students at the outset that they will be writing a monologue based on one of the stories that they hear in class. That announcement guarantees good listening even when the storytelling is less than compelling.

There are several reliable stories that I use, all are highly dramatic life-and-death situations. In one of my stories, I am an exhausted hitchhiker trying to get away from my college town after pulling my fraternity pledge prank. I spend three hours in a car with a driver who is holding a gun. In another tale, my girlfriend and I almost drown in Spain after a huge wave throws us onto a high coral reef where the waves continue to pummel us. In still another story, I give first aid to a camper who has nearly chopped off his leg with an ax. If you search your memory banks, I'm sure you'll come up with a showstopper or two of your own.

I sometimes throw a lot of extraneous information into my stories so that the class begins to distinguish between what is essential, what is simply relevant, and what is totally unnecessary and shouldn't be there. After telling my story, I solicit the class's reaction. It usually takes a little while to get to the critical and analytical part of the discussion, but with a little direction, your class will quickly get the hang of distilling the essential parts of the story from the throwaways. They will also develop an appreciation for keeping a story on course—a tougher job than first imagined. You might want to point out how well good writers are able to this and how very important it is for both the audience and the actors. Art, unlike life, is selected and controlled to maximize its effectiveness; it is never random. Total spontaneity is a reserve of performance.

Once your actors have told their stories and the stories have been thoroughly discussed for their essences, it is time for the second round.

ROUND 2

In this round your students become playwrights. Their assignment will be to adapt into a monologue one of the story events they heard in class. Not all the stories are likely to offer equally strong foundations for building a dramatic piece, so it might be a good idea for you to select five or six with the strongest potential and have your students use only those for Monologue Makers. Narrowing their range of choices will also make clear later, when they perform their monologues, the vast assortment of work that can come from a single dramatic source. During the writing period, it might also be a good idea to read an assortment of monologues in class to provide a model for structure and technique. Analysis of professional monologues can help make clear the dynamics and mechanics of this difficult form of writing.

The finished monologue script should be approximately one minute in length (longer monologues will require too much actor preparation and would probably cause your student playwrights to focus more on quantity than quality). Remind them that their focus, like that of a real playwright, must be on selectivity and control. By using all or parts of one of the events related earlier, each monologue will be adapted by employing much the same process that a professional playwright might go through. To avoid having your students simply retell in their own words one of the stories they heard in class, instruct them that the monologue must not be written for, or spoken by, the student who actually related the event in class. The speaker can be a character referred to in the original telling, or a new character created by your student playwrights. This restriction will ensure that the new script is more than a simple retelling. The playwrights can retain or change the details from the original story to best serve the new work. However, the original event on which the monologue is based must still be recognizable.

Before your students run off to Key West to become Tennessee Williams, it would probably be a good idea to review with them the elements of drama that Aristotle first shared in *The Poetics*. These elements include action, character, dialogue, idea, spectacle, and music. *Action, character,* and *dialogue,* of course, are essential to any dramatic work. *Idea,* or theme, will help glue their work together if they use it and will make the pieces they produce more than simple attempts at entertaining. *Spectacle* refers to any necessary visual and sound aspects. *Music* may literally refer to music in their work (unlikely), or it may refer to the tempo, pace, and even tone of their eventual product.

Action means plot, or what happens in the monologue. This is not the same thing as the events described in the stories on which these monologues are based. Your student playwrights might choose to use only a small part of the overall event first described. However, their one-minute monologue drama must have a throughline of its own, and that's where the interconnectedness of plot and character becomes clear.

For instance, in the event I related about the boy who cut his leg with an ax, the story could be told from several points of view—the wounded camper, the ambulance crew, or the parents of the wounded boy, to mention a few possibilities. The character speaking could also be based on me, the first-aid giver, but many storytelling decisions must be made. Is the speaker the seventeen-year-old boy who had just given first aid? Is he the middle-aged man looking back on this unforgettable event in his life? Who is the speaker talking to and why? How does the speaker change from the beginning of the speech to the end? This last question refers specifically to the throughline of action and means that just as a scene or a whole play must have a forward thrust of action, so, too, must a monologue if it is to be dramatically interesting. The playwright must figure out why his character is talking and create some story progression by creating conflict from the given circumstances that needs to be resolved. The speaker must go through many changes from the beginning of the speech to the end.

The character speaking will be made clear based on what he says and does, so your playwrights must write dialogue that offers clues to the actor who will eventually play the role. The dialogue must demonstrate what the character thinks and feels. Further, playwrights know that dialogue is only one tool for telling the story and revealing character; your student playwrights might want to suggest some actions as well, and even include stage directions.

The idea or *spine* of the play is the theme or themes that connect all the characters and actions together. It is the point behind the play. In life, events are random and seldom connect to each other by a discernible larger plan, but when a playwright or artist shapes her work, she will usually try, consciously or not, to put the world into perspective—to give it meaning. When my camper cut into his leg with an ax, it was an accident. In and of itself, it had no greater meaning than that. But to the playwright, that singular event could be arranged into something far greater. In fact, that young man, after years of ongoing surgery, fully recovered only to later take his own life. Were the events of my story and what I later found out somehow connected? I'll never know, but as a playwright, I could connect those events in a cause-and-effect fashion and, by doing so, provide the spine that might greatly influence the monologue I eventually crafted. Spine is a difficult concept, but it is certainly worth addressing with your students.

Obviously, in a one-minute monologue, spectacle will not and should not be the dominant issue. But where the scene of the monologue is set can be a significant influence in the writing. A private setting requires a different vocal attack than a public one, and the language used in each will certainly be affected. Weather in an outdoor setting can also affect the writing choices as well as its costume considerations. Playwrights have an obligation to picture the scene they are writing about visually and with their other senses too, because ultimately their work is meant to be performed. Playwrights must consider that eventual performance as they write.

Finally, the music of the piece should not be ignored, but it certainly is a sophisticated concept that only the better writers in the class will be likely to tackle seriously. Gifted wordsmiths like Pinter, Shepard, and Mamet use rhythm and tempo consciously to enhance the dramatic power of their dialogue. At the least, you can help your playwrights see and hear rhythm and tempo in the works of great playwrights by exposing them to some. At most, some of your own students might begin to develop an ear for music in their own writing.

When the pieces have been completed, you might have students read their work aloud. Following each reading, the class can react and discuss each monologue's strengths and weaknesses. At this point, the question of tone might come up. Is the monologue meant to be funny or serious? Sometimes a piece can strike the listeners as funny, though the writer didn't intend it to be funny. Is the humor a good or bad thing? Does it work for or against the piece? If it is an enhancement, the writer may want to rewrite with that in mind. If the humor gets in the way, the writer must eliminate what strikes the listeners as funny. This will reinforce the idea that the best writing is rewriting. As any experienced playwright is well aware, a first production of a new play invariably requires rewriting before, during, and after it is rehearsed.

Once the rewrites have been completed, your class is ready for the last round.

ROUND 3

In this round your students will become actors. They are to memorize and rehearse the monologue they have written, selected, or been assigned. I prefer that students not act their own monologues. Since they have been working on the piece all along, by now they probably have too many preconceived notions. Their ability to bring new ideas to the work will be severely limited.

For that reason, doing the monologues of others is probably more beneficial. Seeing others put their own twist on the work is also likely to give the playwrights new ideas for yet another rewrite, should they or you decide it is a good idea. If all the monologues your students have produced are strong enough, you might randomly assign all of them. If not, you might again select the best five or six as you did in the original tellings and pass those out to your students. It usually proves very interesting how an actor's choices can alter what on the page appears so finite and set.

Here is a list of questions your actors might want to consider in their preparation:

Who are you?

Why are you telling your story? (Make your need to tell this story strong and make the need related to the listener.)

Given circumstances? (who, what, when, where)

Who is the listener and why do you need to tell the listener this right now?

What do you need to make the listener do? What do you want from the listener?

Describe the journey your character makes during the monologue. Where are the significant moments in the piece? Where are the moments of victory, defeat, discovery?

How is the listener reacting to the things you say? Where in the monologue do these reactions happen? How can you show that they are happening?

What are the physical actions you can use to help tell the story?

Do you begin and end the piece on the dialogue or on some action? What actions at the beginning and end can help make the story more interesting and clear?

Students then rehearse their monologues and, finally, present their work to the class.

Wrap-up

If your entire class has relied on five or six core story events, the diversity of monologues they produce will be striking. The variety of characters, points of view, tone, and even action will provide your class with excellent subject matter for discussion. Your students will realize that a playwright starts with an infinite number of possibilities from which he must select the ones that will make his story work and, ultimately, give it meaning. Finally, Monologue Makers will provide a solid foundation for a discussion on the playwright as social commentator and philosopher. Most important, it will have brought home the idea that playwriting is an incredibly difficult art and craft on which every actor relies.

Scenes Without Content

At the beginning of each school year I challenge my sophomore scene study class to tell a dramatic and compelling story using only the dialogue "hello" and "good-bye." The purpose of this challenge is to point out to young actors that dialogue is only one of the many tools they can use for telling the story contained within a script. Reliance on dialogue alone seldom produces satisfactory results for the actor or the audience watching. The dialogue a playwright provides is no more or less important than the actions an actor chooses to support the story, whether those actions are implied in the script itself or created by the actor. In either case, it is the physical actions selected by an actor that expresses what a character is thinking and feeling, and what the actor chooses to reveal through those actions is every bit as important as the things his character says. All the given circumstances important to a situation can be implied or clearly stated through action as well, and sometimes making those given circumstances apparent to the audience can mark the difference between work that is believable and clear and work that is not.

In the hello–good-bye exercise mentioned above, the actor is forced to create a set of circumstances that will justify being able to say those two lines in a believable way. Obviously, a set of events must occur after the hello and before the good-bye for that to be possible. If the actor is prohibited from saying any other lines besides those two, then the only other way a story can unfold is through a series of sequential actions that will lead to the eventual good-bye. The possibilities, of course, are infinite. But, by establishing and then making clear a set of given circumstances, the actor considerably narrows his choices. In turn, he can commit to creating a specific story from them.

In a scene from a play, it is all too easy for an actor to simply rely on the dialogue, falsely thinking that the storytelling responsibility lies solely with the playwright. But the playwright writes knowing that she is creating only the blueprint for the director and actors to follow and build upon. Even when a good script is provided, an enormous amount of information remains that must be revealed through the imagination and problem-solving skills of the actor serving that script; common sense, logic, and simplicity become the actor's most precious tools.

Purpose

Contentless scenes like the one mentioned above can provide young actors with the opportunity to use all the basic tools they will need to bring a scene to life. These tools include:

- script analysis
- finding conflict
- using given circumstances
- playing relationships

- playing an objective
- using physical actions
- using risk, high stakes, and obstacles
- creating a dramatic throughline
- recognizing and playing dramatic moments
- listening and reacting
- justifying a line of dialogue

However, because the dialogue does not come from a real play, your actors will not be lulled into thinking that the audience will get the story simply by saying the lines. The fact that there is no information other than the dialogue will force them to put the words they speak into a context, and once they have created that context, they will then have to make sure the audience understands the context they have created.

Obviously, this is not as easy as it sounds. The difference between what is clear to an actor and what is clear to an audience can be like the difference between what is clear to a thinker and what is clear to those sitting around him. Unless the thinker articulates his thoughts, no one will ever understand them. Unless an actor communicates through her actions as well as how she says her lines, no one will understand her. That, then, is the purpose of contentless scenes. They force an actor to make choices about the given circumstances that will justify her dialogue and then to choose actions that can communicate those choices to an audience. The trick, of course, is to choose given circumstances that can be communicated, and "there's the rub," as your students will come to see.

Method
ROUND 1
In the first round of contentless scenes, you might use the hello–good-bye exercise already mentioned, or you might try these alternatives:

SCENE 1
      A: I love you.
      B: I love you too.

SCENE 2
      A: I hate you.
      B: I hate you too.

As you can see, though brilliant, these lines of dialogue do require a bit of fleshing out. Nonetheless, the two scenes suggest a story, however vague. When you first assign these scenes, you might divide your students into pairs and give them about fifteen minutes to discuss what they are going to do with these two lines. Offer no instructions except to tell them they will perform the two-line play.

When your students have regathered, ask for a volunteer pair to perform their scene. In all likelihood, if you offered no more instructions than I suggested, the scenes you see will be vague at best. If the first pair picked the "I hate you" scene, then you might get some yelling and perhaps, if the moon is full, a push or two. What you probably won't get is anything like a clear, compelling story with a beginning, middle, and end. Because "I hate you" suggests conflict, you'll probably get some, but it is unlikely you'll know where that vitriol is coming from.

On the other hand, if the first set of students picked the "I love you" scene, chances are you'll get little more than a generalized sharing of words to that effect. If, by chance, your actors demonstrate some physical affection for each other, be sure to compliment them, because beginning actors can rarely do this. But it is unlikely that the reason for the shared expression of affection will be in any way apparent.

After the first pair performs, allow your entire class to put up their scenes. Following each presentation, ask your students what was good and what was not. Try to direct the discussion so that as the scenes are presented, your students begin to understand that even two lines of dialogue can provide enough foundation for a story. Be sure to ask about given circumstances for each scene (the who, what, when, and where) and try to get your students to define the relationship between their characters. Discuss the importance of conflict in a good story, and get your students to connect the needs of their characters to that conflict. Hopefully, the conflict they come up with will be between their characters. Remind your students that they have now become the playwrights as well as the actors for their scenes. It is, therefore, their responsibility to have the good sense to change the things about their story that simply don't work. Impress on your students that good ideas must be converted to actions the audience can see and understand.

Once all the scenes have been performed, assign the exercise as homework, if possible. Ask your students to rework the scenes they have already put up using the input they have gotten in class. Their goal is to perform a clear and compelling story the second time around. Their rehearsal preparation should include the following considerations:

- given circumstances
- conflict
- high stakes
- objectives
- dramatic throughline
- a story with a beginning, middle, and end

A little procedural note here. I always allow students to use props to make it easier for them to ground their work in reality. It is also important to make it clear that you expect the work your students bring in to be well-thought-out and rehearsed. Further, insist that the work they prepare be realistic, so that they avoid the temptation to go for laughs. Also, make it clear to your students that the point of the exercise is not to do perfect work, but, rather, to develop the ability to think through the implication of each of their choices so that the work they eventually perform is believable, clear, and exciting to watch.

When the reworked scenes are presented, repeat the discussion process from the first presentation. Remind students that solving the problems in the first scene may create new problems in the revised scene. This is part of the trial-and-error process that scene work requires.

ROUND 2

The procedure in this round is the same as in the previous. The only difference is the number of lines contained in the script. More lines mean more complications, however. As with any learning process, mastery comes with time, repetition, and experience. Feel free to determine how your own students best spend their limited time. It is clear to me, however, that the discipline involved in preparing and executing contentless scenes well serves the students when they jump to actual scene work from scripted material.

Below are a number of four-line scenes that I made up. They ain't Shepard or Mamet. They ain't Williams or O'Neill. They ain't even Inge. You can probably do better than I have, and I strongly suggest that you give it a try. But in defense of my own work, please note that each line I have written is intended to suggest and create a transaction between the two characters in the scene. The new information put forth by each character should cause each actor, in turn, to re-evaluate the dramatic situation at hand and their relationship to each other. Because each new piece of information changes the situation as it was previously known, it redirects the story action and each character's attitude about it. The actors must be able to recognize the dramatic information contained in each transaction and then must be able to play them fully while altering their objectives accordingly. In addition, as in a real play script, there are clues in each of these four-liners that will suggest choices to the actors—clues that actors cannot afford to skip over if they are going to fully realize the script for an audience.

SCENE 1
> A: Yo!
> B: How ya doin'? Want some?
> A: Naw. We could get in trouble.
> B: Here.

Using this four-line thriller to teach basic script analysis may prove very effective. Notice the basic conflict suggested here. There is an offer, a rejection of the offer, and a reassertion of the offer—tremendous potential for intensity. Further, there is a suggested finish to the playlet. That final "Here" goes unanswered. Does that mean that under duress the offer was finally accepted? Does it mean a change of heart by character A? Or does it suggest the beginning of a new round of conflict? Which makes the best story? That is the challenge your actors must face and make choices about.

Notice also the actual language used. What type of person says "yo" and "naw?" Does that suggest anything about the character? Remember, your actors must justify everything in the script, including use of the vernacular. Once they determine who might use such language, that may help set up the given circumstances for the action in the scene and help determine what the offered substance is.

Here's another:

SCENE 2
> A: Give me.
> B: Don't, please.
> A: Give it.
> B: Please.

Again in this one, the conflict is clearly present. Unlike in the first, where the conflict is introduced, in this one it is present from the starting gate. Character A wants something that B does not want to give. What is that item that A so badly wants to possess? Notice that A's first line is unusual: "Give me." Why would the playwright structure the line in such a way? Assuming the playwright is no beginner hack, he must have done so for a reason. Notice that A's second line is a variation of the command of the first. Yet this time A says "Give it." What could that "it" be? Your actors will have to find an "it" that justifies those two constructions when they put their scene together.

Now take a look at B's lines. Clearly B is the weaker of the two characters, no attempt at asserting power, whatsoever. Does this suggest anything about the relationship of the two characters? In B's first line, there is a suggestion that A has advanced on B. "Don't, please" suggests that A is doing something to B rather than taking something, as might be inferred by simply reading the first line in isolation. B's second line seems almost like begging when read at the end of the entire sequence. What situation justifies the bizarre syntax of the lines and the obvious difference in power of the two characters? That is the problem for your actors to analyze and resolve.

How about this one?

SCENE 3
    A: You wanna?
    B: Okay.
    A: Do you like it?
    B: Feels good. Good.

This one has no obvious conflict. Therefore making a clear and compelling plot is not as obvious as in the previous two. That does not mean, however, that the actors are not responsible for coming up with a good story. So, here is where good actor-think becomes essential. Look how the script provides the clues when you know how to read it. A makes an offer in the first line. B accepts the offer. No conflict on face value. But who says B accepts the offer immediately? Suppose B must consider before agreeing? Suppose B must consider a lot because the offer is risky, or unpleasant, or unusual? The conflict could be B's internal dilemma, but that doesn't mean the conflict is any less dramatic than if A and B were at odds. The important point is that the actors must come up with something interesting to do. A's next line lets us know that B has accepted the offer, and A is waiting for a report by B on his reaction. B says it feels good. But again, B's report can be far more than simple information giving. What did B go through to ascertain that it "feels good?" Whatever that process is, it offers the possibility of a very interesting sequence of actions, depending, of course, on what the given circumstances are. In addition, notice that B not only reports that it feels good but goes even further. B repeats the word *good*. Handling that second good will provide a lesson for your young actors about dramatic progression. There can be no empty dramatic moments onstage. If the playwright chooses to repeat a word or phrase, he does so to move the story forward. That second good reflects new things unfolding, and the actors must express that progression.

Finally, at least in terms of dialogue, this scene has no resolution. And that will prove unsatisfactory to an audience that has watched the action unfold up to this point. How can the actors reasonably conclude the story? It is up to them to complete their dramatic throughline in a way that will give both the situation and the audience closure. That is an actor's responsibility. Without dialogue, only physical actions can make clear the ending—another good challenge for young actors.

And finally:

SCENE 4
    A: Get down. I said get down.
    B: Cool.
    A: Loser.
    B: Yeh.

This one is difficult but worthwhile. It requires a lot of problem solving, so you might want to save it for a smart pair of actors, or use it only at the end of the unit. In this scene A starts out by giving an order. He has to repeat it. Why? That must be justified by the actors. The fact that an order is repeated twice suggests some danger or at least a high-stakes situation. An order to "get down" is often associated with an attack or an enemy approaching. Yet B's response goes totally the opposite way. B finds the situation "cool." What could the situation possibly be? How can your actors justify through their given circumstances such a bizarre reaction?

The situation then gets even more strange. A calls B a "loser." Why? What has transpired? What has B done to provoke such a response from A? Why does B agree with A's assessment by saying "yeh"? Or is B's response to something other than A? Don't look here for the answers; I don't have them. But your students had better provide you with them. That is the challenge.

As you can see, a tremendous amount of thinking and planning is often necessary to make these scenes work. But it can be a lot of fun solving the acting problems that an imaginative set of given circumstances can provide. Young actors often dig a hole for themselves by creating given circumstances that they cannot make clear. Too often students will stick to these impossible choices even when it becomes obvious that they won't work. For some reason, students fall in love with their choices and continue to use them even when those choices bury them. Contentless scenes make it clear that actors are only obligated to do what the script requires; everything else is up for grabs. Whatever they choose to do in their scenes should be subject solely to rule number one: Use it only if it works.

LATER ROUNDS

As with the first round of scenes, the exercise is more worthwhile if performed twice. The process of getting feedback and translating that feedback into choices that work is incredibly important. So is a disciplined rehearsal process to integrate and perfect the new choices, as well as improving the moment-to-moment acting transactions.

You may want to analyze the scripts with your classes before assigning the work, or you may want to save the analysis as a response to the unclear, unjustified work they bring in the first time. Either approach seems valid to me. I prefer the latter because, invariably, students bring in work the first time certain they have a terrific scene. Their shocked response to the blank reactions they get is often priceless. But in either case, the real work is accomplished in the follow-up discussions and in the rehearsal process.

Wrap-up

Contentless scenes provide a setting that encourages actors to do all the preparatory brain work necessary for good acting. Detective skills are required in the script analysis of a play to uncover the character motivation often hidden behind dialogue that, to a young actor, may seem to drive itself. In contentless scenes, however, the actor is not lulled into thinking his work is already done for him. As a result, he must use all the tools of the craft, but only after he has made the preliminary decisions that are essential for good work. And getting the young actor to realize this makes contentless scenes a worthwhile exercise.

Afterword

Several years ago, an interview in *Vanity Fair* caught my attention. Journalist David Halberstam had managed to get the reclusive box office superstar Harrison Ford to sit down with him for an interview. At the time, I had just begun working on an article that several years later would develop into my acting textbook, *The Actor as Storyteller* (which, by the way, makes a wonderful companion to *Head-First Acting*). What I read in that interview not only delighted me but reinforced the ideas that ultimately became the cornerstones for the acting approach offered in that book and the one you are reading now. What Ford kept returning to in that interview was that he saw his job as that of a storyteller—no more and no less. It was his job, he felt, to figure out what his character was doing at every moment of the story and to find ways to communicate that clearly to the audience so that the overall story would be properly told. "My God!" I thought at the time, "He sees it the way I do!" I felt as elated at that moment as if I had discovered a vein of gold.

Until I had read the interview with Ford, I had never heard anyone but myself talk about acting in that fashion, yet it had become obvious to me that in the most successful theater productions and films, storytelling is exactly what all members of a production team do. On the other hand, I had discovered that a seemingly good performance could ruin an excellent script by failing to serve that story in the proper manner. My definition of good acting—acting that is believable and tells the best possible story while serving the script—grew out of this simple recognition. More important, I had discovered that this approach to acting worked wonderfully well with my own students, mostly beginners of high school age.

Seven years later I had nearly completed *Head-First Acting*. I had been struggling to find a way to tie the writing together, but I wasn't sure how to conclude a book of acting exercises. While brainstorming futilely, I noticed that Harrison Ford was going to be interviewed by James Lipton on "The Actor's Studio." I was struck by the symmetry in this and sensed that my writing had brought me full circle.

In his introduction, host James Lipton referred to Harrison Ford as one of film's "masters of acting craft," and in several clips from some of his most successful movies, Ford clearly proved Lipton's case. In the selected clips, many of them with little or no dialogue, Ford employed the acting craft in ways that parallel closely many of the points that are emphasized throughout the exercises in this book. Furthermore, Ford expressed that his approach toward acting is planted in the concept of "actor as storyteller."

A viewer need only watch *Air Force One* or *The Fugitive* to see how this is so. In both films, Ford played out scenes in which the audience must know what his character is thinking and feeling without benefit of dialogue. In some of the best scenes, where Ford's character is either alone or hiding from enemies, not a moment goes by in which the audience is not following his every thought and feeling with total understanding. That, of course, is craft—selection and control of physical actions chosen and developed to communicate specifically the story from moment to moment to an audience.

The sequence of exercises in this book are intended to produce such results, or, at the least, an awareness that such results are possible for every actor willing to embrace craft and develop it. The journey toward performance begins with an understanding of the story or script an actor works from—whether created by the actor himself or provided from an outside source.

Understanding the conflicts and converting that understanding into choices that can be seen clearly by an audience is what the best actors do at every moment. It is also one of the purposes behind each of the exercises found in *Head-First Acting*. Finally, the ability to listen to fellow actors onstage and temper individual choices in accordance with the give and take from moment to moment is what Ford does all the time. It is also the final aspect actors must address in every piece of work they put onstage when they are not acting alone.

Head-First Acting explores all these ingredients and their finer points through the exercises. A mastery of each exercise sequentially can fully prepare the beginning actor for more sophisticated script work. By the time your students tackle their scripts, whether during or after their explorations in *Head-First Acting*, they will have wrestled with and overcome many of the challenges they will continue to face as they pursue their goal of mastery in acting. Please keep me posted about the journeys you and your students make through theses exercises, and let me know what discoveries you have made on your own. I look forward to hearing from you, and hope you will share with me some of what you have learned during your explorations.

Glossary

Action Any physical or psychological activity an actor carries out; the throughline of action in a play.

Analysis and synthesis The intellectual tools necessary for breaking down and putting a play back together so that it will work effectively for an audience.

Beat The length of script during which an actor plays a single objective.

Beginnings, middles, ends The necessary steps that an actor must go through for all effective storytelling.

Blocking The physical elements of storytelling onstage—movement, gestures, and business.

Business Any ongoing activity an actor carries out while completing an acting task onstage.

Conflict When two opposing forces meet; the engine of all drama; the core ingredient an actor must recognize before choosing an objective.

Craft The tools of acting that can be learned and mastered; unlike talent which is innate.

Defeats The moments onstage when an actor as character discovers his objective cannot be won. This moment will be followed by a transition.

Discoveries Any new information that an actor as character learns—information that should be reacted to.

Emotional memory The use of personal memory to create an emotion that can be used in an acting situation.

Emotional truth The product of an actor who can find and produce honest emotions within himself that serve the acting situation he is engaged in.

Endowment Giving an object specific emotional meaning that can be effectively used for acting purposes.

Gesture A single specific physical action that communicates emotion, information, or attitude.

Given circumstances The who, what, when, and where of a play or scene that must be considered before making acting choices.

Head-first acting A term coined by the author to suggest that good acting requires analysis and synthesis and that the best choices are ones that serve the story. These choices must be thought out rather than simply intuited.

Indicating When a performer physically demonstrates what she is supposed to be thinking, feeling, or doing.

Intention Another word for the acting objective or action an actor pursues.

Journey The combined series of changes an actor undergoes as a character while pursuing his overall objectives (can also be referred to as *throughline* or *arc*).

Justification The process an actor goes through to make sure that a line or moment is acted in such a way that it is both believable and clear and makes sense in the given circumstances of the situation.

Listening A basic requirement for an actor if she is to be believed, and an essential step for staying in the moment and reacting effectively.

Magic if, The An acting term coined by Stanislavski that reminds an actor to ask, "What would I do if I were the character in this situation?"

Method, The An internal approach to acting centering on the use of emotional truth and sense memory; heavily used by Lee Strasberg but based on early writings of Stanislavski.

Moment The smallest unit of dramatic action that can be acted.

Moment-to-moment Refers to the ability of the good actor to respond to what an acting partner is saying and doing at a particular moment.

Motivation The reason behind a character pursuing a particular objective. Motivation cannot be played directly but can be used as a device to find the objective.

Movement Traveling from one place to another onstage.

Negative choices Tactics used by an actor that keep him from getting what he needs. These should be avoided.

New information Anything a character finds out onstage that can change what she thinks, feels, or does. Something that an interesting actor will usually respond to.

Objectives The needs an actor playing a character must pursue at all times onstage.

Obstacles The things in a scene or play that keep a character from obtaining his objective. They provide conflict and heighten the stakes of an acting situation.

Personal space A setting over which a character has privacy and control. No one is permitted there without the owner's approval.

Physical action The tangible and visible things a character does onstage.

Positive choices The choices an actor makes in pursuit of her objective that actually help her get that need fulfilled.

Private space An acting setting to which there is limited access. Not everyone is permitted to go or be there, as opposed to public space.

Public space An acting setting in which all people are free to use, to come and go, and to observe each other.

Relationship An acting tool used to help define the dynamic behind a particular relationship.

Risk A basic acting tool for producing interesting acting; the more risk taken, the more interesting the actor in a situation.

Sense memory The use of personal memory relating to smell, sound, taste, touch, and sight to enhance the emotional power of an acting moment or situation.

Selectivity and control Qualities necessary for the creation of all good art. Acting choices must be thought out and contribute to the story being told; spontaneous choices do not necessary do so.

Spine The central idea that interconnects all parts of a script and holds it together.

Stakes The things that are at risk for the actor that make the acting situation more interesting.

Stanislavski, Constantin The Russian theater director, actor, and teacher responsible for most of the basic craft used in actor training.

Strasberg, Lee The famous American acting teacher who developed The Method.

Substitution A technique in which an actor substitutes a parallel personal memory for a similar one in the play he is working on to enhance his emotional connection to a moment.

Tactics The specific things an actor as character does while pursuing her objective.

Tangible The things an actor does that can actually be seen by the audience. Most often these are physical things.

Throughline The combined series of actions that are mapped out in a script by an actor as he works out his character's story moment by moment, scene by scene (also *journey* or *arc*).

Transitions The actable moments when one objective is given up and replaced with another. This transition occurs as a result of an objective being lost, won, or abandoned because of a new information, interruption, or discovery.

Victories The actable moments when objectives are reached.

Bibliography

Aristotle. *Poetics*. Translated by Kenneth A. Telford. Chicago: Gateway, 1968.

Barton, Robert. *Acting: Onstage and Off*. Fort Worth: Harcourt College Publishers, 1993.

Bentley, Eric. *The Dramatic Event*. Boston: Beacon Press, 1954.

―――. *The Life of Drama*. New York: Atheneum, 1964.

Brook, Peter. *The Empty Space*. New York: Atheneum, 1968.

Bruder, Melissa, et al. *A Practical Handbook for the Actor*. New York: Vintage Press, 1986.

Clurman, Harold. *On Directing*. New York: Macmillan, 1972.

Cohen, Robert. *Acting One*. Palo Alto, CA: Mayfield Publishing, 1984.

Felnagle, Richard H. *Beginning Acting*. Englewood Cliffs, NJ: Prentice-Hall, 1987.

Hagen, Uta. *Respect for Acting*. New York: Macmillan, 1973.

McGaw, Charles, and Larry D. Clark. *Acting Is Believing*. Fort Worth: Harcourt College Publishers, 1996.

Meisner, Sanford, and Dennis Longwell. *Sanford Meisner on Acting*. New York: Vintage Books, 1987.

Miller, Bruce J. *The Actor as Storyteller*. Mountain View, CA: Mayfield Publishing Company, 2000.

Moore, Sonia. *Training an Actor.* New York: Penguin, 1979.

Silverberg, Larry. *The Sanford Meisner Approach.* Lyme, NH: Smith and Kraus, 1994.

Stanislavski, Constantin. *An Actor Prepares.* Translated by Elizabeth Reynolds Hapgood. New York: Theatre Arts Books, 1936.

———. *Building a Character.* Translated by Elizabeth Reynolds Hapgood. New York: Theatre Arts Books, 1949.

———. *Creating a Role.* Translated by Elizabeth Reynolds Hapgood. New York: Theatre Arts Books, 1961.

Whelan, Jeremy. *Instant Acting.* Cincinnati: Betterway Books, 1994.

with logical choices that focus on the most important and interesting elements of an unfolding story.

Method

Tell your students that they will be doing a group improvisation. Tell them they have found themselves together away from civilization, in a cabin with one large community shower space with several shower heads. There is no place to hide. Tell them that when the exercise begins, they must quickly shower and dress. Make time an important element so they will not avoid getting into the shower for too long. Begin the exercise and see what happens.

Discussion

This improvisation is intended to be a stop-and-go exercise in which your observation and coaching is a critical element. The acting concepts you will probably spend the most time on include the following: logical sequence (Does this action follow logically from the previous one?), objective and focus (Do the actors play objectives that are consistent with what is most important in the moment?), justification (Are the actions that occur supported by the given circumstances established?), and the "magic if" (If I were the character in this situation, how would I behave?).

To some extent this exercise is a trick, especially if you do it following extensive work on The Solo Shower exercise. After focusing so hard on making a story out of the ordinary ingredients of shower taking, most of your student actors will probably focus on their showering process rather than the big dramatic element of the situation—the fact that they're all standing around together naked. Start the exercise and let it go on for a while. When you stop to discuss, eventually ask why so many of them ignored the fact that they are seeing each other naked for the first time. Many will probably rationalize their explanation, but just keep hitting them with the "magic if." Each time your actors redo the exercise, more of them will deal with the

About the Author

Bruce Miller is the Interim Chair and the Director of Acting Programs for the Theatre Arts Department at the University of Miami, where he teaches acting, directing, and script analysis. His stage productions have received many citations, including the Moss Hart Award for "most outstanding production" by the New England Theatre Conference. He has been a recipient of the E. E. Ford Foundation Award for Teaching Excellence and has been recognized two times by *Who's Who Among America's Teachers*. He has taught acting workshops nationally and internationally and most recently has been conducting Professional Development Institutes in the Teaching of Acting for the Educational Theatre Association. His articles on acting appear regularly in *Dramatics Magazine* and *Teaching Theatre*, and his textbook on acting craft, *The Actor as Storyteller*, has recently been published by Mayfield Publishing Company. He is a member of AEA, SAG, and AFTRA and holds an MFA in acting from Temple University. Mr Miller is available for lectures and workshops and can be reached at brucejmill@aol.com.